And Ye Shall Know the Truth

by

James L. Giles

ISBN 1-56229-425-3

A Division
of
New Life World Ministries

In Memory
of
Isaac Lamar Rogers
1966-1992

Acknowledgements

To the Father, the Son, and the Holy Spirit without whom this project would still be a wish.

I pay homage to all the scholars and scholar-prophets who have gone before and to those who are yet lifting pen and voice in behalf of justice and mercy-Habari Gani.

To my wife Shelley and my sons Cedric, Armand, Stephen, and Langston (Four Future Kings). Thanks for your patience and understanding. You are the center of my life-Ujima.

To my parents James and Greta Giles who sparked my love for learning. I love you!

To Joan Capdeville Cook, my aunt, a very special lady who has always believed in me and encouraged me. Whatever success I achieve you are largely responsible.

To the Giles and Cook families and my grandmother Eleanor Cook and Great Aunt Rubye Cook-Hunt.

To Charletta Ann Gibbs who typed and retyped this manuscript.

To the Sons of Issachar.

To the New Life Family Christian Center for your openness to Biblical truth, your commitment to unity, and very importantly for your ability to laugh, love, cry, and rejoice. You have helped me to grow in ways hard to explain.

To Professors Albert Black and Sarah Vandenberg of the University of Washington for encouraging me to write early on. Also for exemplary scholarship and for their commitment to teaching.

To Pastors Tony and Rene Morris; Dr. Leonard and Pastor Varnise Lucas; Prophet Bernard and Prophetess Debra Jordan and Dr. Myles and Ruth Munroe for your support and encouragement.

To Obery M. Hendricks for our fertile discussions at Princeton in the Spring of 1989 and for your continued support.

This book is lovingly dedicated to the memory of Ethel Giles and Louis Herman Cook; my paternal grandmother and maternal grandfather.

Foreword

In the United States of America, children are generally required to begin their official education around the time they reach five years of age. This "formal"educational process involves the development of thought and concept concerning a wide variety of topics. History happens to be one of those topics.

The historical perspective of this educational process normally includes national and world history. This would appear to give a person brought up in this environment a good vantage point of different races and cultures. Their significant investments and contributions to humanity as a whole would also be included. Unfortunately this has not been the case. Therefore generations of people in this process have been taught to view history and historical events a particular way. This way has not always been advantageous or accurate concerning all people.

The history of a person and a people not only influences their present but often predicts their future. This happens because history is to be one of our greatest teachers in life. So if it has been inaccurately told or not told at all that person or people will inevitably face much confusion about who they are. Throughout the Bible, God would frequently have His people look back before He took them forward. This would give them the vitality they needed to face their future. Without an understanding of who you are and where you have come from, the risk of perpetuating wrong or failure is extremely high.

This has been the case with many people throughout the world. In this country African-American people have been particularly affected. Often the effects have been measurable by the definitive attitudes of inferiority and hopelessness. This must change and can change with a reeducation in biblical and academic history based upon truth.

In this book, Pastor James Giles approaches these issues with much research and comprehension. "And Ye Shall Know The Truth," is a part of the reeducating of not only African-American people but all people. Pastor Giles explores a broad horizon to bring centralization of information that often has not been discussed. "And Ye Shall Know The Truth," is a must read for educators, politicians as well as church leaders. The type of information that is presented in this book will be vital to the restoration of a people and lead them into the twenty-first century with a proper knowledge of who they are and what they can do. I believe that this book will leave a legacy for many generations to come.

Pastor Tony Morris
Seattle, Washington

Authors Introduction

This book has been a labor of joy and sorrow, laughter and tears, but definitely a labor of love. It is dedicated to the millions of misdirected people of African descent across the globe. From Seattle to Detroit, New Orleans to Los Angeles, from Washington, D.C. to Trinidad, from Ghana to the Bahamas. This is a love gift to every African-American male wrestling with the media images that offer him no dignity; to every African-American woman who believes her prospects for marrying a caring, sensitive African-American male are slim. It is for everyone who finds solace in the crack pipe and for every gang banger who can bring himself to wound or kill another brother over turf.

This book is for every African-American who has been taught that African people have made no significant contributions to the world's history. May you be stirred and provoked to throw off the mantle of sloth and indifference. I say boldly to every African-American boy or girl searching for images of greatness among his or her own people. You can chart the stars and plumb the ocean's depths. You can understand and explain elegant mathematical theorems. You can perform delicate surgeries and understand arcane philosophies. You can master physics, earn a law degree, develop innovative software, graduate summa cum laude. You can pilot a 747, design a shopping mall, coach the Super Bowl winning team, win Wimbledon, become a Morehouse professor. You can excel in the sciences, design an environmentally friendly car or truck, pilot the space shuttle, become a pioneer in education, give the commencement address, become a successful entrepreneur. You have the seed of greatness within you. It is the gift of God. I hope your seed will be watered as you read and learn of the exploits of your ancestors. May the light of the Son shine upon you and give life to the seed of greatness within you.

This book is also for my white brothers and sisters. For you need to know the truths contained in this book every bit as much as any African-American. I have had to stand before you and teach these truths only to watch you judge me presuming to know my heart. Don't worry, I understand how you must feel. Let's pray for one another. You should learn these truths and teach them to your children, families, peers, and friends. Ask for a Bible study in your church that teaches you to esteem the history and accomplishments of all peoples. Above all my white brother and sister do not continue to walk in division of the Body because of your unwillingness to allow God to free a people's minds and spirits. This is a precious time of refreshing for many in the African-American segment of the Body of Christ. You should share the rejoicing!

Contents

ONE

In the Real Beginning

Do you know that prosperity is the legacy of the Black man, the brown man, the red man, the white man, and of all men? I mention the Black man first because it is with him that history properly begins. Prosperity, as I use it, is not some contemporary fad teaching, neither is it a heretical substitute gospel. Prosperity is the promise of God; the covenant promise of God to bless the whole of man's personal, political, economic, and social relationships. Prosperity is the promise of righteousness, joy, and peace in the Holy Ghost. It is the promise of the Kingdom of God. It is the blessing of God upon the creative dimension of man. There are several Biblical words for prosperity, prosperous, prosperously, etc. . Here are some of them from the Old Testament with their meanings. (1.) Tsaleach (tsaw-lay-akh): to push forward; to break out; to break out mightily; to be profitable (2.) Sakal (shaw-kak): to be or act intelligent or circumspect; to be skilled, expert, prudent; to have good success; to teach or have understanding, or wisdom; to guide wittingly (3.) Shalom (sha-lome): to be safe, well, friendly, happy, peaceful, healthy, and whole (4.) Tselach (tsel-akh): to advance, promote, or prosper (5.) Towb (tobe): the widest sense of good; beautiful, gracious,

1

or well- favored; prosperous; ready, sweet, most merry; wealthy (6.) Shalam (shaw-lam): to be safe in mind, body, or estate; to be completed, finished, made full; to perform prosperously; recompense; to make restitution, restore, or reward.

However Satan, through crafty strategies, the greed and deceitfulness of men, and the deception of mankind, has stolen from us our legacy of wealth, dignity, and nobility. The very first prosperous man was an African, his name was Adam. The Bible locates the Garden of Eden in Africa. Genesis 2:10-14 says: "And a river went out from Eden to water the garden; and from thence it was parted, and became into four heads. The name of the first was Pison: that is it which compasseth the whole land of Hav-i-lah, where there is gold; and the gold of that land is good: there is bdellium and the onyx stone. And the name of the second river is Gi-hon: that same is it that compasseth the whole land of E-thi-o-pia. And the name of the third river is Hid-de-kil: That is it which goeth toward the east of Assyria. And the fourth river is the Eu-phra-tes."

Concerning the African origins of civilization, the eminent British paleontologist Louis S. B. Leakey wrote, "Africa was the birthplace of man himself, and that for many hundreds of centuries hereafter, Africa was in the forefront of all world progress." Michael Carter, in his book "Archaeology," wrote: "Africa can perhaps be described as the cradle of mankind - the birthplace of man." Sir Godfrey Higgins, in his scholarly work "Anacalypsis," wrote: "Now I suppose that man was originally a Negro..."

God turned all of creation over to Black (African) Adam to "dress it and keep it." What awesome responsibility born of God's trust in Black Adam. The garden represented God's best, it was good. Concerning Adam's blackness, Dr. Eric Womack has written; "The word *hama'a* is an Arabic word that describes the dust of the ground. It denotes Black, Black Mud, Black Clay, Sound Black Mud,

2

Black Moulded Loam. Adam's body was fashioned from all the elements that formed the earth. His body was moulded from water and carbon. He was not fleshly pink or sandy beige. His material composition was allowed to dry (baked) in the sun. The Creator (Almighty God) breathed in this Black shell and it became a living soul." How have the African and the African-American nations been so radically separated from this noble legacy? These African people have a heritage of unbroken communion with God which comes from Black Adam before his expulsion from the garden. Black Eve was part of this communion, this fellowship, inasmuch as she was created from the rib of Adam by the direct intention of God, not as an afterthought. It is important to note that Eve's name was Adam before the fall. So when God calls for or mentions Adam before the fall He is referencing the male and female, the one Adam.

Not only did God entrust all His wealth, His real estate, gas, oil, gold, silver, onyx, and bdellium to Adam; He also turned over to him the plant and animal kingdoms and blessed him with a profound intellect. In Genesis 2:19-20 we find Black Adam giving us the science of zoology.

As we in America strategize to liberate the African-American male from staggering unemployment, underemployment, crack-cocaine addiction and nihilism born from lack of vision and purpose we need to be reminded that Black Adam was the first human to work. His work was God ordained. His work was meaningful, His work was worship. Genesis 2:15 (NIV) says, "The Lord God took the man and put him in the Garden of Eden to work it and take care of it. "Eden is from the Hebrew word *enuah* which means pleasure or delight, or to live voluptuously. The Lord placed Black Adam in the garden of pleasure and delight. Pleasure, because of the American obsession with superficial "fun" and expensive self indulgence, has become a negative term to many serious thinkers. However,

3

an examination of many Biblical passages will prove that as a balance to productive, worshipful work, God rewards us with some rest and leisure. Pleasure, rest, and re-creation, are gifts from God.

The Bible is the most conspicuous authentication of the Black genesis of civilization. Study Genesis 4 and you will discover the Black Man building cities, farming, developing animal science, the metal working arts, smelting, and music and unfortunately murder and treachery. However, destiny does not end there. We also know that the Black man was the first man in recorded history to enslave other human beings. It was the Black Egyptians who enslaved the Israelites. Later African tribal kings sold their brothers and sisters into slavery participating in the cruel inhumanity of the Atlantic Slave Trade. Even in the streets of Urban America we must stop blaming Black on Black crime on whites. Whites are not threatening to imprison us if we refuse to murder one another. Are our people smoking crack at the end of a white person's gun barrel? Do not misunderstand, I am sensitive to the spiritual and psychological effects of institutional racism. However, God and His Word constitute ultimate reality, not racism or white people. It is time to stop externalizing blame and get a vision for the rebuilding of America's decaying inner cities. The Japanese rebuilt their people and nation in the aftermath of Hiroshima and Nagasaki. They did it with vision, hard work, determination, faith, and of course reparitions. Three of those four are available to us, thus the odds are in our favor. Black people have been building and rebuilding since the beginning. We were so successful on one occasion that God had to personally intervene to prevent our success (see Genesis 11:1-8).

We all know the story of the flood and how God spared one preacher of righteousness named Noah and seven of his kin folk . The Bible informs us that Noah's sons procreated more sons. Once again, after the flood God entrusts the earth and the redemption of humanity to the Black Man. Genesis 9:1 says, "And God blessed Noah and his sons, and said to them, be fruitful and multiply, and replenish the earth." Once again, the command to populate the earth is given to the Black Man. There is copious archaelogical and anthropological evidence that the earliest civilization began in Africa, moved up the Nile, out through the Isthmus of Suez, through Southern Italy into Asia and Europe as it is known today. Fossil evidence cited by such scholarly giants as C. A. Diop and L. S. B. Leakey place the first man in Africa about 5,500,000 years ago and Homo Sapiens or man essentially as we know him in Africa about 150,000 years ago. Though many Dispensationalist theologians and preachers date the earth at approximately 6,000 years old, much of science based upon Carbon-14 dating places the earth much older than 6,000 years. We acknowledge the suspicions regarding both Carbon-14 and Dispensationalist dating. Whichever method we choose however, still places the Black Man at the beginning of civilization.

C. A. Diop, the Pharoah of African Studies, writes in the "African Origin of Civilization," " Throughout antiquity the Meroitic Sudan was even believed to be the birthplace of man." Diop quotes Champollion Figeac's travelling companion Cherubini, "The human race must have been considered there as spontaneous, having been born in the upper areas of Ethiopia where the two sources of life-heat and humidity are always present. It is also in this region that the first glimmerings of history reveal the origin of societies and the primitive home of civilization. In the earliest antiquity, before the ordinary calculations of history, a social organization appears, fully structured, with its religion, laws and institutions." Cherubini also says of the Ethiopians, "...They boasted of having preceded the other people on earth and about the real or relative superiority of their civilization while most societies were

5

still in their infancy...."

In "The World and Africa," W. E. B. DuBois wrote, "If we follow inherent probability, ancient testimony, and legend, this would seem to have been the history of Northeast Africa: In Ethiopia the sunrise of human culture took place, spreading down into the Nile Valley. Ethiopia, land of the blacks, was thus the cradle of Egyptian civilization. Beyond Ethiopia, in Central and South Africa lay the gold of Ophir and the rich trade of Punt on which the prosperity of Egypt largely depended."

George Washington Williams, a Baptist minister, the first Black to be elected to the Ohio state legislature, and the first African-American to write a history of Africans in America from the inside, wrote in Volume I of "History of the Negro in America:" "Before Romulus founded Rome, before Homer sang, when Greece was in its infancy, and the world quite young, "hoary Meroe" was the chief city of the Negroes along the Nile. Its private and public buildings, its markets and public squares, its colossal and stupendous gates, its gorgeous chariots and alert footmen, its inventive genius and ripe scholarship, made it the cradle of civilization, and the mother of art. It was the queenly city of Ethiopia - for it was founded by colonies of Negroes. Through its open gates long and ceaseless caravans, laden with gold, silver, ivory, frankincense, and palm oil, poured the riches of Africa into the capacious lap of the city."

Now let us look again specifically at the Bible. God populated the world after the flood through the sons of Noah. Geneseis 10:5 says, " By these (Noah's sons) were the isles of the Gentiles divided in their lands; every one after his tongue, after their families in their nations." Genesis 6:10 is important because it records the Blackness of Noah's generations. " And the sons of Ham; Cush, Mizraim, and Phut, and Canaan. And the sons of Cush; Seba, and Havilah, and Sabtah and Raamah and Sabtecha:

6

the sons of Raamah; Sheba and Dedan. And Cush begat Nimrod; He began to be a mighty one in the earth. He was a mighty hunter before the Lord. And the beginning of his kingdom was Babel, and Erech, And Akkad, and Calneh, in the land of Shinar."

Genesis 10 again shows the Black Man building kingdoms and "great cities" specifically in verses 8-32. In Genesis 10 we see God not only replenishing the earth through the Black Man, but also giving mankind language, the concept of kinship ties, families and nations. In "The History of the Ancient World" Volume II, M. Rostontzeff, one-time Professor of Ancient History at Yale University, wrote, "The ancient civilization, which spread by degrees over the world, was first developed in the near east and chiefly in Egypt, Mesopotamia....In this civilization there were successive epochs of high development...a series of creative periods which produced inestimable treasures not only of a material kind but also in the intellectual region of culture....The zenith of culture was attained by Egypt and Babylon in the third millenium B. C. and again by Egypt in the second millenium." By about 4,000 B. C. the Sumerians had attained a high level of civilization in southern Babylonia. The Sumerians built cities, raised cattle, practiced irrigation, tilled the soil, and developed a system of writing which they passed on to the succeeding so-called Semites or Afro-Asiatics. We are told that when the Greeks discovered Babylonian science over four-thousand years after this period they could not improve upon it.

In "World Civilizations," Burns and Ralph declare that "The mother of most ancient civilizations was that which began in the Tigris-Euphrates valley as early as 4,000 B. C. This civilization was formerly called the Babylonian civilization. It is now known however, that the civilization was not founded by either the Babylonians or the Assyrians but by an earlier people called the Sumerians. It seems better, therefore, to use the name Mesopotamia to cover the whole civilization." The Sumerians were Black and can be traced back to Cush and Ethiopia. Burns and Ralph add, "More than to any other people the Mesopotamian civilization owed its character to the Sumerians." Black Sumerians built prosperous cities in Mesopotamia.

Here we should note that the first man to whom the Bible refers to as being wealthy, the first man to cut the blood covenant with God was a Black Man. His name was Abram later changed to Abraham. Abraham lived in Ur of the Chaldees with his family. Genesis 11:27-28 says, "Now these are the generations of Terah: Terah begat Abram, Nabor, and Haran; and Haran begat Lot. And Haran died before his father Terah in the land of his nativity in Ur of the Chaldees." According to George Rawlinson in "Five Great Monarchies of the Ancient Eastern World," "the first Chaldeans were predominantly Kushite...In Susiana (Elam), where the Kushite blood was maintained there was, if we may trust the Assyrian remains, a very decided Negro type of countenance. The head was covered with short crisp curls, the eye was large, the nose and mouth in the same line, the lips thick. In another work, "The Origin of Nations," Rawlinson wrote, "A laborious study of the primitive language of Chaldea, led him (Sir Henry Rawlinson) to the conviction that the dominant race in Babylonia at the earliest time to which the monuments reached back was Kushite or Ethiopian." Upon quick reading there would seem to be an inconsistency between Nimrod's building of Babylon as the first Biblical kingdom and pre-Babylonian Sumer. However, a quote from Runoko Rashidi should resolve the conflict. Rashidi writes, "Ancient Sumer, which has been called Shinar, (Genesis 10:10) Chaldea, Babylon, and Babylonia, is the first major high culture of Asia. Extending over southern Mesopotamia, it has in fact been projected as the birthplace of the civilization itself. This conclusion however, would appear to be the result of a combination of simple ignorance and scholastic racism. Sumer actually seems nothing less than a Nile Valley offshoot, its citizens calling themselves the Blackheads." (Nile Valley Civilizations; Ed. Van Sertima 1985) It is from among the Black Chaldeans of Ur that Abram is called by God into Egypt. God created Black Adam, he disobeyed God and was expulsed from the garden, the place of God's covenant, protection, and sovereign will for Adam and the human race, the race intended by God to subdue and have dominion over the earth. All the world's nations or ethnic groups have come from the loins of Adam. We truly whether black,red, yellow, brown, or white are all of one blood.(Acts 17:26) God caused it to rain for forty days and forty nights upon the earth but saved righteous Black Noah and his sons. However, once again evil proliferated in the earth and God was disappointed. Though God was disappointed, He made a covenant with Noah to never again destroy the earth by flood. Now God had another plan and He calls upon Black Abram to assist Him . Listen to God's word to Abram found in Genesis 12:1-3: "Now the Lord said unto Abram, get thee out of thy country, and from thy kindred and from thy father's house, and unto a land that I will show thee: And I will make of thee a great nation, and I will bless thee and make thy name great; and thou shalt be a blessing. And I will bless them that bless thee, and curse him that curseth thee: and in thee shall all the families of the earth be blessed." God is going to bless every family, every nation, ethnic group or tribe through Black Abram. It is our divine destiny to bless humankind as is evidenced by the scientific, philosophic, and religious contributions of our fathers and mothers in Cush, Ethiopia, Egypt, Europe, Russia, and the U.S.

Let us not lose sight of the emphasis of this work, namely to establish prosperity broadly speaking , as the legacy of the Black race. God called Abram into Egypt in the time of famine and he emerged wealthy. Genesis 13:1-2 says, "And Abram went out of Egypt, he, and his wife, and all that he had, and Lot with him into the south. And Abram was rich in cattle, in silver and gold." Black Abraham, being rich was also the first person in the Bible to tithe. Genesis 14:18-20 says, "And Melchizedek king of Salem brought forth bread and wine: and he was the priest of the most high God. And he blessed him, and said, "Blessed be the most high God, which hath delivered thine enemies into thine hand. And he gave him tithes of all."

Black Man, it is your legacy to be called of God. You are a builder of cities and of great empires. God has called you at pivotal points in history to bring salvation and deliverance to humanity. Just as Satan has attempted to destroy your father Abraham through political and military intrigue and deviant sexual practices; and your other leaders through countersubversion, deceit, sin, and murder, so today he plots our destruction. However, ours is a history of resilience and grace and we are raised up for this hour. Satan will not defeat us.

God is calling and supernaturally equipping you and me. We must esteem our scholars and teachers past and present. Resurrected from purposelessness, we must rise and redeem the souls of a people, many of whom do not even realize they are in bondage. God is straightening our backs and causing our faces to be like flint. Our homes and communities bemoan physical, psychological, spiritual, and social death while Satan hisses his sick twisted approval. Many upon whom God has placed the call to the ministry are being destroyed by the lies of Satan. But the hour has come saith the Lord when I shall find the men, and I shall indwell them. The world will marvel as they arise. They shall arise from the waste places, from the barren places. Their voices shall be given authority. I shall establish vision in their hearts. They shall drink from the wells which Abraham digged. No longer will I allow them to be relegated to inferiority. I will give them a measure of influence in the world and in the Church and they shall lead with boldness and compassion saith the Spirit of the Lord. Through them I will begin to redeem the waste places and they shall be looked upon with favor. They shall be apostles and prophets who will guide the Church of Jesus Christ. Ye shall know that I am with them. For now shall come forth Nehemiahs and I will send them to the waste places where there is rubble and decay and they shall build. They shall not be alone; for there shall be chains of influence around the world. And you shall not concern yourselves with finances. For I will give you favor with men and much wisdom saith the Spirit of the Lord. This is a prophetic word spoken to me by the Lord as I was writing in the early morning hours of December 17 , 1991. There is a strong urgency in my spirit concerning this word. Before it will come to fruition it must be connected with our Biblical history and spiritual purpose and destiny.

Do not mistake the obvious emphasis upon the African-American male for sexism or machoism. For the male is the seed-bearer. Mass infanticidal attempts under Pharaoh and Herod in Scripture were intended to destroy male (seed-bearing) infants. No other group in the history of the world has experienced such a sustained and demonically ingenious psychological and spiritual warfare as the once kingly African-American male. Robert Staples in "Black Masculinity" wrote, "...In the Black community, it is the men who need attending to. They are the ones who are failing in school, losing ground in the labor market to white and black women, filling up the prisons and dying slowly through drugs, alcohol, violence and adventurism." I might also add that the African male is grossly underrepresented in the most recent Kingdom census.

The multiple warheads of western pseudo-science, falsified history, anglophiliac hermeneutics, and Euro-slave christian praxis have conspired to dethrone the kingly, priestly African-American male. Robbed of his God-given dignity and leadership inclinations and of his ability to dream and envision God's promises for his life and generation he sinks into a pathological self-hatred and destructiveness.

The African-American male is the Lazarus of American society and he must experience a resurrection. Many of our men, young and old, are stinking in the grave of modern plantations called ghettoes or in modern parlance "Urban Communities." Others are the victims of the opprobrium of cultural deception. As one very astute member of our congregation puts it "...Church is one of the most dangerous places to be Black." Not that the goal of life is to see how black one can be. Ethnicity is a point of self-definition and should be embraced and celebrated as a gift along with the ethnic and cultural gifts of others. You must know however, that the Blackness to which he alludes is not simply an issue of skin color. My brother is dealing with the larger issue of that which makes one unique culturally. The Church must cease the attempt to impose a vanilla standard on all believers. We must begin to appreciate the special giftedness of every nation, kindred, tribe, and tongue. The church is to be spiritually homogenous while ethnically and culturally diverse.

Pseudo-integration into the American mainstream has narcoticized the minds of many Blacks and members of other ethnic groups. By touting an ambiguous notion known as Americanism this culture has the unique ability to seduce ethnic peoples into cultural suicide. This is a dysfunctional denial of self and is completely foreign to the Scriptures. Blinded by the shallow and destructive value system of capitalist consumerism many Blacks and other ethnic peoples in America have adopted a "hear no evil" "see no evil" approach. Right Wing conservative Christians in America are also to blame as they uncritically endorse American domestic and foreign policy which is greedy, dehumanizing and perpetuates a status-quo in which the rich get richer and the poor get poorer. In America there should be no such thing as a permanent underclass. A posture of non-engagement and the acceptance of non-solutions has led minimal advance relative to critical issues such as racism, which because they exist and determine the fate of millions of men, women, and children daily, should be at the top of the Church's agenda. Souls are crying for release from these urban (Inner Cities) of bondage. Jesus said "...ye shall know the truth , and the truth shall make you free." It is the truth that will liberate our African-American, Native-American, Mexican-American, Asian-American, and so-called Third World brothers and sisters and ultimately our entire nation and world. The Church in America must repent and summon the courage to be confronted by truth.

The Apostle Paul wrote in II Corinthians 5:17, "Therefore if any man be in Christ, he is a new creature: old things are passed away; behold all things are become new." Any so-called gospel which does not allow us to "be in Christ" that is to authenticate ourselves culturally with dignity, must be rejected. The Jew must be allowed to "be in Christ," so must the Black, the Asian, the Native-American, and the European. Contrary to some contemporary logic based upon American race paranoia, this appreciation for ourselves and others will not produce greater separation and division. Really, how much more divided can we be? After all Christ, whose ethnicity we shall establish in a later chapter would encompass all ethnic groups just as in light theory all colors on the light spectrum when merged become Black. We must seriously scrutinize what it means to be an American. Notions of unity and patriotism which masquerade as spiritual and radical while remaining lukewarm on issues of justice must be rejected because of their hypocrisy. The Gospel of Jesus Christ was not born in a western context and in fact much of western Christianity, specifically American Church polity and theological praxis, is an affront to the prophetic traditions of both the Old and New Testaments. Any so-called gospel which calls for docility and apoliticism while we watch our communities self destruct must be rejected.

We must publicly condemn the ignominy of "Planned Murderhood," decry the violence of unemployment, underemployment, welfare, and diminishing healthcare availability, crack-cocaine addiction, disproportionately high infant mortality and incarceration rates, AIDS and the general despair which plagues America's Urban Communities. We must call into account African-American brothers and sisters who abuse their platforms as star athletes or entertainers by peddling cigarettes and alcohol into our communities. Business executives and advertising moguls profit from these ventures while Black people get cancer, emphesema, hyper-tension, jail time, broken families and broken bank accounts. Black people who can least afford these genocidal commodities spend inordinate amounts of money on them. In many cases when these people lose their jobs often due to alcohol and drug related declines in performance levels, they may spend portions of their unemployment or welfare monies purchasing these addictive substances. In many cases this misappropriation of funds deprives other family members of basic subsistence needs. If every Black person in the world stopped smoking cigarettes and consuming alcohol tomorrow it would seriously injure many enterprises in America which can only prosper as long as Blacks wish to kill themselves.

If Winston tastes good like a cigarette should then let Mr. Winston smoke them all. Let him chain-smoke his own little lung-decaying dynamite sticks. If consumption

14

of some alcoholic substance confers royalty then let the manufacturers of such substances be duly coronated. Brothers and sisters we need deliverance and it is not going to come through injesting deadly substances. We must began to pray, to cry out to God for creative and Biblical strategies of spiritual and social rebirth.

TWO

Ethiopia and Egypt (Cush)   (Mizraim)

Cheikh Anta Diop has written that "...The history of Black Africa will remain suspended in air and cannot be written correctly until African historians dare to connect it with the history of Egypt."

The word Cush is prominent in the Old Testament. It appears four times as the name of a person (Genesis 10:6,7,8 and Psalm 7) with the Genesis account being duplicated in I Chronicles 1:8,9,10. Cush is mentioned as the first son of Ham and the father of Nimrod. This would make Cush the ancestor of various people located in Africa and Southeast Asia. The introduction to Psalm 7 refers to Cush as a Benjamite. It reads, "Shaggaion David, which he sang unto the Lord concerning the words of Cush the Benjamite."

Other forms of the word Cush appear throughout particularly the Old Testament. They are Cushan, Cushan-reshathaim, Cushi, Cushite, and the Cushite. Cush means "black-skinned" people. The word Cush is translated into Greek as Ethiope or Ethiopia, Ethios-meaning burnt or black, ops meaning faces.

In Numbers 12:1, the Bible tells us that Moses married a Cushite or Ethiopian woman. This was not a so-called miscegenous marriage. Moses certainly was not caucasian. In Jeremiah 38:7,10,12, Ebed-Melech, an officer in King Jehoiakim's court is described as being Cushite or Ethiopian. This brave Cushite is traditionally said to have rescued the Prophet Jeremiah from an abandoned well into which he had been dumped by the political establishment under King Zedekiah.

The Cushite presence goes on. In II Samuel 18:21,32 David has a Cushite courier in his army. The general's couriers are always men of the utmost integrity, presence, and ability. Another later example of the high esteem with which Ethiopian soldiers were held is attested to by the attempt of Hyksos king of Apophis about 1600 B.C. to persuade an Ethiopian Pharaoh Kamose. Apophis promised to divide Egypt with the Ethiopian ruler and history leaves us to question the Ethiopian's response. Egyptians and Ethiopians (Nubian, Cushites) have fought together well in the twentieth century.

It was the strong military leadership of Kashta and his son Piankhi that began and finished the conquest of Egypt in the eighth century B.C. It is said that the independent Napatan Kingdom of Kush completed its conquest of Egypt at about 730 B.C. Piankhi and his successors constituted the Twenty-Fifth or Ethiopian Dynasty which ruled Egypt and occupied an area extending to the shores of the Mediterranean for about sixty years.

In 693 B.C. Tarkaka son of Piankhi conquered the entire Nile Valley. He was welcomed by Memphis and Thebes where he established his capitol.Tarkaka's Kingdom extended from the Pillars of Hercules in the west to Assyria in the east. Tarkaka was driven out by the Assyrians in 670 B.C. the twenty third year of his reign.

In Jeremiah 36:14, "Cush" appears as the name of the great-grandfather of Jehudi who also was a member of King Jehoiakim's court. In Zephaniah 1:1, the Bible says, "The word of the Lord came unto Zephaniah the son of

Cushi, the son of Gedaliah, the son of Amariah, the son of Hizkiah, in the days of Josiah, the son of Ammon, king of Judah." Hizkiah is one of the English transliterations of Hezekiah. Strong's Exhaustive Concordance of the Bible would lead us to believe that there was only one Hizkiah or Hezekiah in the Bible. Hezekiah was king of Judah from 715-686 B.C. He was among at least five kings of Judah noted for righteousness. The other four were Asa, Jehoshaphat, Uzziah, and Jotham. Hezekiah ascends the throne at twenty five years old. He forsakes the idols of his father Ahaz and purges Judah of its idolatry. Cushite blood courses through Hezekiah's veins.

In addition to referring to individuals by Cush or its derivatives, Ethiopia/Cush appears six times naming a land located in some instances south of Egypt. Ethiopia is mentioned in Genesis 2:13 as the place around which the River Gihon flows. In Esther 1:1; 8:9, Ethiopia/Cush appears as one of two boundaries of the Persian empire. Isaiah 18:12 refers to "the land shadowing with wings, which is beyond the rivers of Ethiopia: That sendeth ambassadors by the sea...." Ethiopia/Cush is also mentioned by Ezekiel and Isaiah, Ethiopia/Cush is also spoken of by Amos, Zephaniah; Jeremiah, who pronounces a blessing upon Ebed-Melech for saving his life, Nahum, and Daniel. Cush/Ethiopia is very important in the Bible and world history.

According to W. E. B. Dubois, the Greeks had a legend which located Ethiopia on "either side of the Red Sea in Africa and Asia....The Sudan was known to the Egyptians and Hebrews as Kush or Cush. In Hebrew folklore, the descendants of Ham "were Cush and Egypt." (Dubois 1965) Historian John G. Jackson has written, "A number of scholars both ancient and modern have come to the conclusion that the world's first civilization was created by a people known as the Ethiopians (Cushites)." (Jackson 1970) According to Herodotus, the Father of History, and

18

Homer, both of whom wrote favorably of Ethio-pian/Cushites; these people inhabited the Sudan, Egypt, Arabia, Palestine, Western Asia, and India. Lady Lugard in "A Tropical Dependency" wrote: "The fame of the Ethio-pians was widespread in ancient history." Herodotus de-scribes them as "the tallest, most beautiful and long lived of the human races" and before Herodotus, Homer in even more flattering language, described them as "the most just of men, the favorite of the gods"...while they are described as the most powerful, the most just, and the most beautiful of the human race, they are constantly spoken of as black...the leading race of the Western world was a black race." Ethiopian/Cush is also referred to as Meroe and Mirakh. Meroe became the capital city of the Kingdom of Cush (Ethiopia) in the early part of the sixth century B.C. replacing Napata. The Meroitic Kingdom lasted until sometime between the end of the third and the middle of the fourth century B.C. In Book II (sec. XXIX) Herodotus refers to Meroe as "...a big city named Meroe, said to be the capital city of the Ethiopians." Meroitic Kushites over time developed their own distinctive writing, created a distinc-tive style of architecture, and were prolific ceramists. Their pottery has been recognized as being some of the most beautiful and artistically valuable ever produced.

Chancellor Williams in his brilliant work "The De-struction of Black Civilization," wrote: "The land of the Blacks was a vast land, a big world unto itself covering 12,000,000 square miles. From its northern most point in what is new Tunisia to Cape Aqulhas is approximately 4,600 miles. The whole of this second largest continent was once Bildad as Sudan, "The Land of the Black," and not just the southern region to which they had been steadily pushed from the north. After Asian, Greek and Roman occupations, the term "Sudan" came to indicate the areas not yet taken from the Blacks and was co-extended with the Ethiopian empire."

I would again like to quote Sir Godfrey Higgins from "Anacalypsis" Vol I: "I shall, in the course of this work, produce a number of extraordinary facts, which will be quite sufficient to prove, that a black race, in very early times, had more influence in the affairs of the world than has been lately suspected; and I think I shall show, by some very striking circumstances yet existing, that the effects of this influence have not entirely passed away."

Here again we assert evidence of the Blackness of Ham and his progeny. In Hebrew, Ham is Kham; son of Noah; Khum: or chestnut, Khom: or heat: Khama; or the sun. In ancient Egyptian, Ham is Khem which means black or burned or Ham which is hot, black. In Wolof, which is a tongue spoken by the Senegalese, Khem is black or burned. Thus such Afrocentric scholar/teachers as Molefi Kete Asante refer to Egypt as Kemet or Khemet, the land of the Blacks or burnt faces.

The Old Testament scholar John Patterson tells us in "The Bible and History" that, "No other land is mentioned as frequently as Egypt in the Old Testament....To understand Israel one must look well into Egypt." Egypt is the word Mitzraim in Hebrew. Mitzraim or Mizraim is a compound which refers to Upper and Lower Egypt. (Genesis 10:6). This word along with its cognates occurs some seven hundred forty times in the Old Testament.

In their language the Egyptians had one term to designate themselves: Kmt or literally the negroes. According to C.A. Diop, this term is the strongest term in the Pharonic tongue to denote blackness: The Biblical word Ham or Kham is derived from this word. There are also in the Pharonic tongue other words denoting Blackness. Kmtjw or the Black man was the word which is also the Egyptians. Here we see that in the Pharonic tongue Black and Egypt are synonymous. Also they are Rmt Kmt, or the men of the country of the black men; Kmit, or the whole people of Egypt. In Kmit there are two symbols in the Pharonic, one for man, another for woman. Both symbols are subsumed under the designation of black. The ancient Egyptians clearly referred to themselves as Black.

You and I are both aware of the insidious plot on the part of white racist capitalists, supported by Euro-slave Christianity to caucasianize Egypt. This is perhaps most arrogantly represented by American film culture's casting of a very white Elizabeth Taylor in the role of a very Egyptian or Khemitic (Black) Cleopatra or Charleston Heston as Black Moses. Whites have re-historized history and taken credit for contributions they not only did not make but could not have made. The historical record strongly establishes that when Cush (Ethiopia) and Mizraim (Egypt) were at the zenith of their development caucasians were in a barbaric or semi-barbaric state in Europe. In fact there was no Europe as we know it in ancient times. Scholars such as Diop suggest that the first European was Grimaldi Man, an African who migrated to Europe only about 150,000 years ago.

According to certain Carbon 14 dating Cro-magnon man, the first caucasian appears about 20,000 B.C. Diop places Australapithicus at about 5,500,000 years. Australapithicus was a Black African.

Gloger's law posits that warm-blooded animals evolving in a warm climate will secrete a black pigment called eumelanin. Therefore, if mankind was born in the tropics of Africa, he would have had black pigmentation from the start. The earliest men could only have moved out from Africa through the Sahara and the Nile valley. As these men moved out into Europe and Asia and into colder climates, modification of Gloger's law would explain differences in skin pigmentation, eye color, and hair texture.

The testimony of antiquity also established the Blackness of Cush/Mizraim through its classical writers. Herodotus, Aristotle, who has been venerated for formulating philosophic concepts which can be proven to have been

21

stolen from Egypt, the Greek writer Lucian and Appollodorus who wrote, "Aegyptos conquered the country of the black footed ones and called it Egypt after himself."

The geographer Strabo, Diodorus of Sicily, Diogenes Laertius, and Aminianus Marcellinus and the authoritative Volney all attest to the Blackness of early Egypt. Volney who visited Egypt between 1783-1785 wrote, "...ancient Egyptians were true negroes of the same stock as the autochthonous peoples of Africa and...one sees how their race after some centuries of mixing with the blood of Romans and Greeks, must have lost the full blackness of its original mould."

Bishop William Montgomery Brown wrote in "The Bankruptcy of Christian Supernaturalism:" Vol. II, "For the first two or three thousand years of civilization, there was not a civilized white man on the earth. Civilization was founded and developed by the swarthy races of Mesopotamia, Syria, and Egypt, and the white race remained so barbaric that in those days an Egyptian or a Babylonian priest would have said that the riffraff of white tribes a few hundred miles to the north of their civilization were hopelessly incapable of acquiring the knowledge requisite to progress." R.R. Palmer and J. Carlton in "A History of the Modern World" wrote, "Half of the record of history had passed before anyone in Europe began to keep written records between 4,000 and 3,000 B.C."

C.A. Diop writes, "...the Indo-Europeans never created a civilization in their own native lands: the Eurasian plains. The civilizations attributed to them are inevitably located in the heart of Negro countries in the southern part of the Northern hemisphere: Egypt, Arabia, Phoenicia, Mesopotamia, Elam, India. In all those lands, there were already Negro civilizations when the Indo-Europeans arrived as nomads during the second millenium." (Diop 1974)

Joseph McCabe, an English scholar wrote, "Four thouoand years ago, when civilization was already one or two thousand years old, white men were just a bunch of semi-savages on the outskirts of the civilized world. If there had been anthropologists in Crete, Egypt, and Babylonia, they would have pronounced the white race obviously inferior, and might have discoursed learnedly on the superior germ plasm or glands of colored folk." (McCabe, "Key to Culture")

I. Khamit-Kush has written, "...even after the Greek (and thus the Romans) were civilized by the Africans in Egypt most of what we know as "Europe" was still barbaric and unheard of."

The entire history of the world must be rewritten with the Black man taking his rightful place as the forerunner of civilization. The names of Cheikh Anta Diop, George G.M. James, W. E. B. Dubois, Chancellor Williams, John G. Jackson, William Leo Hansberry, Marcus Garvey, Malcolm X, Granville T. Woods, Elijah McCoy, Jeanne Craig Sinkford, Dorothy Lavinia Brown, Alexa Canady, Benjamin Carson, Carter G. Woodson, and Ivan Van Sertima must be as familiar in our minds as those of Dr. Martin Luther King, Jesse Jackson, Michael Jordan and Michael Jackson.

THREE

Contributions of Ethiopia and Africa

The geographical area known as present Sudan in antiquity was known as Nubia. It was in Strabo's Geography that Nubia appears for the first time to designate the land which the Greeks called Ethiopia. Ethiopia in the Greek language means burnt face.

In the Pharonic language nwb (Nub) means gold and Nubia was very rich in the precious metal. Nubia in ancient Egypt was referred to as Ta-Seti (Land of the Bow). The greatest area of African concentration was Nubia and it was there where the great civilization which was extended over Egypt was developed. Though the achievements of Egypt are the most carefully recorded among the African nations, we know that Kush, Nubia, and Ethiopia developed much independent of Egypt and contributed much to Egypt's grandeur.

The inhabitants of South Egypt had ancestors who originally came from Somaliland and entered the Nile through Nubia. In Somaliland, building remains have been discovered which closely resemble the architectural style of early Egypt. When these Africans migrated out of the Nile Valley perhaps earlier than 5,000 B.C., they possessed weapons and tools of iron.

24

Of this tool making W. E. B. DuBois has written that it began in the Nile Valley sometime during the reign of Menes or Narmer which began between 3200 B.C. and 3180 B.C. DuBois writes: "The first tools were stone, the eolita and the stone ax. Then came metals: copper, especially from Nubia and then iron. This tool making and artificing in stone and other metals allowed for more sophisticated methods of agriculture and also for the development of weapons technology."

I mentioned earlier that the Egyptians had in their own tongue one designation for themselves, Kmt or the Blacks. Gaston Maspero has written of the Egyptians: "...According to the almost unanimous testimony of the ancient historians, they belonged to an African race which, first established in Ethiopia on the Middle Nile, gradually came down toward the sea, following the course of the river. To demonstrate this, one relied on the evident analogies between the customs and religion of Meroe (Ethiopia's capital) and the customs and religion of the Egyptians proper. Today we know beyond the shadow of a doubt that Ethiopia, at least the Ethiopia known by the Greeks, far from having colonized Egypt, was itself colonized by Egypt..."

The Pharaoh of African Studies, C.A. Diop had written, "Egypt (Ham, Mizraim), Ethiopia (Kush), Palestine and Phoenicia before the Jews and Syrians (Canaan), Cerabia Felix before the Arabs (Pout, Hevila, Salia) were all occupied by Negroes who created civilizations thousands of years old in those regions..."

The great French Egyptologist Abbe' Emile Ame'lineau (1880-1916) who discovered among other notable excavations the tomb of Osiris at Abydos has written: "From various Egyptian legends, I have been able to conclude that the populations settled in the Nile Valley were negroes, since the goddess Isis was said to have been a reddish-black woman. In other words, as I have explained, her complexion is cafe' au lait (coffee with milk), the same as that of certain other Blacks whose skin seems to cast metallic reflections of copper."

Ame'lineau further states, "...Egyptian civilization is not Asiatic, but of African origin, of Negroid origin, however...We are not accustomed, in fact, to endow the Black or related races with too much intelligence, or even with enough intelligence to make the first discoveries necessary for civilization yet there is not a single tribe inhabiting the African interior that has not possessed and does not still possess at least one of those first discoveries."

You might ask what those first discoveries were. According to Ame'lineau a Black race called the Anu created in prehistoric times all the elements of Egyptian civilization. Among these developments were the practice of agriculture, the building of dams, invention of writing, art, science, the calendar and the irrigation of the Nile Valley.

We are discussing the contributions of Egypt and Ethiopia (Nubia). Before the invasion of Egypt by Alexander II (the Great) in 332 B.C.E. and the subsequent partitioning and ruling of Egypt by the so-called Ptolemies, Egypt was known by its indigenous Black African population as Ta-merry, Sais, etc. Ethiopia or Nubia was known as Ta-Nehisi or Itiopi, and all of the Motherland or Africa was known as Alkebu-lan. Ancient Egypt was also known as the Pearl of the Nile.

For centuries there has been an effort on the part of European and Euro-American "scholars" to caucasianize Egypt and to parcel the entire continent of Africa of which Egypt was a part so as to minimize African world influence. This is simply the kidnapping of history on the part of these so-called scholars and the institutions and interests they represent. This kidnapped history has been held hostage for over four hundred years by the worldwide racist, white supremacy stronghold.

Joseph B. Danquah, a Ghanaian historian, has written, "By the time Alexander the Great was sweeping the civilized world with conquest after conquest from Chaeronia to Gaza, from Babylon to Cabul; by the time the first Aryan conquerors were learning the rudiments of war and government at the feet of the philosopher Aristotle: and by the time Atheus was laying down the foundations of European civilization, the earliest and greatest Ethiopian culture had already flourished and dominated the civilized world for over four centuries and a half." (Lapido Solanke 1927)

E. A. Wallis Budge in his book "Egypt" says: "The prehistoric native of Egypt, both in the old and new Stone Age, was African..." Budge further states; "There are many things in the manners and customs and religions of the historic Egyptians that suggest that the original home of their prehistoric ancestors was in a country in the neighborhood of Uganda and Punt."

The breadth and depth of Egyptian culture is well chronicled by African, African-American and European scholars. In the "Ruins of Empires," Count C. F. Volney writes that the Egyptians were the first people to "attain the physical and moral sciences necessary to civilized life."

Leonard Jeffries Jr., in a review of C. A. Diop's "Civilization or Barbarism" (1981) states: "In so far as Egypt is the distant Mother of the science and culture of the West, Diop points out that this book will reveal that the major proportion of the ideas we consider foreign are often modified, turned over and perfected images that were the creations of our ancestors: Judaism, Christianity, Islam, the Dialectic, the theory of being, exact sciences, arithmetic, geometry, mechanics, astronomy, medicine, literature (novel, poetry, theater), architecture, arts, etc." (Van Sertima 1986, 1989)

That which has come to us from antiquity in the name

of Greece was stolen from Egypt when Alexander II (the Great) of Macedonia conquered her in 332 B.C.E. Aristotle and other so-called Greek philosophers stole multitudes of volumes from the Grand Lodge of Luxor (Thebes) and plagiarized Egyptian texts.

In the September 1980 edition of the "Journal of African Civilizations" Dr. John Pappademos, professor of Physics, University of Illinois at Chicago Circle, states that the "Greeks generally viewed Egypt as the seat of scientific knowledge."

Professor Beatrice Lumpkin in the same issue of JAC writes; "The same sort of talents that brought together a centralized government in Ancient Egypt, that constructed the vast network of irrigation canals, that developed the first phonetic writing and embedded an alphabet into beautiful picture writing, wrote the first medical treaties, composed a body of literature and phenomenal art that we still admire today, that invented the first ciphers to represent numbers-these were the talents that underlay the ability to create the awe-inspiring pyramids, obelisks and temples."

In an article reviewing Martin Bernal's "Black Athena" Basil Davidson, himself a copious writer on things African wrote: "The Greeks all agreed upon the cultural supremacy of Pharonic civilization, and the ways in which they wrote about this clearly show that they would have thought it deserved to advance a contrary opinion." Davidson further states: "For the Greeks of the Classical Age, Egypt was where one went to learn history."

At about 10,000 B.C.E. (before the Christian Era), man's first calendar was developed along the Nile River Valley. The first Solar Calendar ever made by man was introduced in 4100 B.C.E., the Grand Lodge of Luxor (Thebes) was built at Danderaly by Pharaoh Khufu during the IIIrd Dynasty.

The Grand Lodge of Luxor (Thebes) was the world's

first university. It was originally 2,000 feet long and 1,000 feet wide at its base. Both Greeks and Romans visited the Grand Lodge of Luxor where the highest levels of learning could be obtained. It was here that the Greeks and Romans were introduced to Philosophy, Religion, Mathematics, Law, Engineering, Science, Medicine, History, and Astronomy.

The Grand Lodge of Luxor had chapters the most notable of which was at Kharnak. Kharnak was built one half mile from the Grand Lodge. The two edifices were connected by a magnificent walkway sixty feet wide and a half mile long. Separated each by twelve feet was a double row of sphinxes on either side of the walkway. At the height of its influence the Grand Lodge housed an elite faculty of priest-professors, catered to an estimated 80,000 students at various grade levels and housed over 700,000 volumes. Luxor was destroyed by fire in the year 548 B.C.E. It is believed to have been burnt down by envious foreigners.

In his work, "A History of Science," George Sarton wrote: "It is childish to assume that science began in Greece. The 'Greek miracle' was prepared by millennia of work in Egypt."

It is interesting to note also that of the so-called Seven Wonders of the World described by ancient Roman writers only the pyramids of Egypt have survived into the present. Colonel Alexander Braghine wrote in "The Shadow of Atlantis:" "A detached study of the structure (of the pyramids of Egypt) will convince any investigator that the wealth of mathematical, geometrical and astronomical data concealed within it is not accidental."

John G. Jackson in "Introduction to African Civilization" writes: "It seems that the knowledge of mathematics and astronomy among the ancient Egyptians was considerably more extensive and exact than we had hitherto been led to suspect."

The discovery of the Ishango bone in Zaire (Congo) over 8,000 years ago evidences a mathematical system in Africa. Though the bone was found in the lakes region, it is possible to trace the Ishango people through their bone harpoons down the Nile Valley by commerce or migration. History informs us that so-called Egyptians did not read or write until some 2,000 years after the discovery of the Ishango bone. The Ishango bone has been called the oldest scientific document.

We know that the Ta-Merrians (Egyptians) of Akebulan (Africa) taught the Greeks mathematics.

In "The Ancient History," Sir J. G. Wilkinson wrote: "I have also known that Herodotus and others ascribe the origin of geometry to the Egyptians but the period when it commenced is uncertain. Anticledes pretends that Meoris was the first to lay down the elements of that science, which he says was perfected by Pythagoras; but the latter observation is merely the result of the vanity of the Greeks, which claimed for their countrymen (as is the case of Thales and other instances) the credit of enlightening a people on the very subject which they had visited Egypt for the purpose of studying." Thales has been credited by Greeks and the west with having been the first to study geometry from Egypt to Greece. Over fifty years after Thales (c.-600) visited Egypt to study geometry Pythagoras (Pythagorean Theorem) spent twenty years in Egypt and Mesopotamia. Democritus (c.-400) also studied in Egypt. Euclid of Alexander lived and died in Egypt. Erastosthenes, the first man to accurately measure the earth's circumference was a Bubasite born in Libu or a Libyan born in Libya.

Again we consult the brilliant Professor Beatrice Lumpkin. She informs us that: "Menelawa of Alexandria (c.-100) laid the foundation for spherical trigonometry and its application to astronomy." Professor Lumpkin further states: "In this same period, the mathematician and engi-

30

neering genius Herod of Alexandria, invented 100 machines and wrote extensive mathematical works" (ed. Van Sertima, 1985 reprint, 1989).

Cheikh Anta Diop, the late Pharaoh of African studies wrote: "The Rhind papyrus shows that the Egyptians did invent the arithmetic and geometric progression. It is interesting to note that the most famous "alleged" discoveries of Pythagoras deal with geometric and arithmetic series. All the operations that he made-summations in particulars-were commonly made by the Egyptians." ("Great American Thinkers" Vol. I, ed. Van Sertima 1989). We also know that the Egyptians, these great Blacks from Ta-Merri in Alkebu-lan, gave us algebra.

The Ta-Merrians (Egyptians) also gave us the science of mechanics as witnessed by a prototype glider plane from about the fourth or third century B.C.E. which hangs in the Egyptian Museum at Cairo. This glider was discovered by Dr. Khalil Messiho in 1969.

The Ta-Merrians (Egyptians) invented steel, the iron smelting furnace, created the first alphabet, originated the use of paper, created architecture, art and as I mentioned earlier gave the world its first university. Sir Godfrey Higgins in "Anacalypsis" declared, "We have found the Black complexion or something relating to it whenever we have approached the origin nations."

One cannot discuss the contributions of Ta-Merry (Egypt) without correcting one of the great historical inaccuracies of the western world. The western world has acknowledged Hippocrates as the "Father of Medicine." This is absurd, the true "Father of Medicine" was Imhotep also known by the Greeks and Romans as Aesculapius. He lived more than two thousand years before Hippocrates was born. Imhotep was known among the Ta-Merrians (Egyptians) as the "God of Medicine" and the "Prince of Peace." In addition to being a medical practitioner Imhotep was the architect who designed the Step Pyramid of

31

Sakhara for Pharaoh Djoser (Zoser) in the IIIrd Dynasty (c.-2789-2689). The Step Pyramid was the first of the Colossal Pyramids. Imhotep was also a poet and Prime Minister.

Count C. F. Volney in the "Ruins of Empire" wrote: "Egyptians priests always regarded the preservation of health as a point of the first importance indispensably necessary to piety and service of the gods."

According to the Ebers papyrus the Egyptians discovered blood circulation and the function of the heart. In the Smith papyrus there are detailed descriptions of several cases of brain injury. The works of Imhotep which were housed at Memphis were consulted in the fifth century B.C.E. by Hippocrates and until the second century B.C.E. by Theophrastus, Dioscorides and Galen. It is believed that Theophrastus along with Eudemus and Andronicas both of Rhodes, formed the triumvirate of rogues who assisted Aristotle in beginning the grandest scheme of plagiarism known to the world. They were known as the Peripatetic School.

Robert S. Bianchi, author of "Museum of Egypt" has written of the Ta-Merrians: "The fame of the Egyptians as physicians was well-known in antiquity. Darius the Great (521-486 B.C.) mightiest King of the Persian Empire, enlisted an Egyptian as his personal physician and is reported to have founded a school of medicine at the Egyptian city of Sais in the Delta."

The Greeks began traveling to Egypt for learning education around 525 B.C.E. This followed over five thousand years of Egyptians prohibition against the Greeks. Greeks could not have learned philosophy in Greece inasmuch as the same was deemed socially, political, and religiously unacceptable. The government at Athens delivered serious punishment and persecution to those convicted of dabbling in the Egyptian religio-sciences and philosophy. Socrates was executed; Anaxagoras was imprisoned and later exiled; Plato was sold into slavery, Aristotle was indicted then later exiled, and Pythagoras was banished to Italy.

George G. M. James in "Stolen Legacy" quotes C.H. Vail from Ancient Mysteries" "Egypt was the center of the body of ancient wisdom, and knowledge, religious, philosophical and scientific spread to other lands through student Iniates. Such teachings remained for generations and centuries in the form of tradition, until the conquest of Egypt by Alexander the Great, and the movement of Aristotle and his school (The Parapetics) to compile Egyptian teaching and claim it as Greek Philosophy." Professor James himself states: "The school of philosophy, Chaldean, Greek, and Persian were part of the Ancient Mystery System of Egypt." (George G. M. James 1985 ed.)

John G. Jackson in "Man, God, and Civilization" wrote: "Egypt from the earliest times had been the university of Greece."

Herbert Wendt in "In Search of Man states: "So great was the achievement of the Africans in the Nile Valley that all the great men of ancient Europe journeyed there--the philosophers Thales and Anaximander, the mathematician Pythagoras, the statesman Solon and an endless stream of historians and geographers whose works are all based on Herodotus' outstanding description of Egypt, to which the second volume of his history entirely was devoted." It is important to note here that Herodotus the Father of European History (ben-Jochannan 1970, 1972) described the Colchians, Ethiopians, and Egyptians as Black and Wooly Haired. "Histories" Book II chapter 57; Book chapter 104).

It is of no mean consequence that Galileo was also influenced by the Egyptians via the Greeks. Galileo had a profound influence on Sir Isaac Newton whose atomic theory held away for close to a century. One of Galileo's heroes was Archimedes who also is reported to have spent time in Egypt.

John Pappademos, Professor of Physics at the University of Chicago has written concerning Egypt's influence. In "Nile Valley Civilizations" Pappademos writes, "The influence of Africa made itself felt in Galileo's experimental work...Galileo certainly helped to establish the validity of the heliocentric theory of the solar system by using the telescope he contructed to observe the phases of Venus as well as the phenomenon of sunspots, but seldom have the prior experiments of Ihu-al-Hattham (Alhazen) of Egypt on lenses been given credit. Alhazen (died in Cairo 1039 A.D.) was one of the greatest optics of all time."

Also the works of Nicholas Copernicus, Johannes Kepler, Rene Descartes and Sir Isaac Newton were not without Egyptian influence.

If the magnanimous, often foundational contributions of Egyptian Priest-Scholar-Philosophers had been recognized by European and Euro-American historians there would in one sense have been no need for continued stream of works such as this. However, the work of C. A. Diop, George G. M. James, Yosef A. A. ben-Jochannan, W. E. B. DuBois, William Leo Hansberry, Author Stromberg, J. G. Jackson, Beatrice Lumpkin, James Brunson, Na'im Akbar, John Hope Franklin and others has been a brilliant sunrise after a long dark night.

There has still not been an official cease-fire declared on the part of European racists who continue daily to hurl the salvos of pseudo science and falsified history at the minds of America's children. Jesus declared, "And ye shall know the truth, and the truth shall make you free." (John 8:32) The Master, Jesus Christ also proclaimed in John 8:36, "If the Son therefore shall make you free, ye shall be free indeed." These two statements of Jesus tells us unequivocally that Jesus uses truth to free people. He would not consent to the manner in which Western culture and Euro-slave Christianity have used His name and twisted his teachings into a demonic ideology of domination.

Egypt, once known as the light of the world, is part of that great expanse the ancients knew as Alkebu-lan, or after the Greeks, Africa. This is the great expanse once dubbed by the Europeans, the "Dark Continent." If the continent was dark at all it was because beginning in 332 B.C.E. with the Greeks and continuing until today Europeans and Americans have stolen its light culturally and intellectually. This book is not intended to suggest a pure and holy history of Ethopia or Egypt. Because of ungodliness and idolatry Egypt is often found under the judgement of God in Scripture. However, the redemption of Egypt is promised by God.

It is time that the "Light of the World" Jesus Christ arises upon Alkebu-lan and her distant children. Jesus said in John 8:12, "...I am the light of the world: he that followeth me shall not walk in darkness, but shall have the light of life."

The darkness that Alkebu-lan and her children have known is the darkness of 2,323 years of standing offstage watching Europeans receive curtain calls for art, science, mathematics, mechanics, music, theater, philosophy and religion that belong to Alkebu-lan and her children.

Jesus Christ is our Liberator. He is Christus Victor! He is not the white man's god. He has loosened the chains from our bodies and minds. He yearns to free us completely from the hegemony and lies of European anti-history. We must drink deeply at the well of truth. Our legacy is noble. It would be absurd to posit an Alkebu-lan, a Ta-Merri or a Ta-Nehisi, an Orphye without sin. There were periods when the Motherland was rife with civil war, economic and political intrigue, fetishism and polytheism. Nevertheless, God the Father's mercies endure forever. Strangely enough the sin of a country or nation does not obscure its scientific, technological, philosophic, and political achievements. One need only look at Europe and the

United States. It is absolutely time for the truth to be told concerning the biblical destiny of the black man and his often favored place in history.

The noble legacy of Alkebu-lan will allow us, African-Americans, Spanish and Spanish-Americans, Asians and Asian-Americans, and European Americans, all of whom have traces of Alkebu-lan in their blood, to seize our noble destiny, and to become God's chosen Nation, His Royal Priesthood. God's anointing upon noble legacy will empower us to conquer poverty, drugs, unemployment, broken homes, undereducation, miseducation, inferiority, and spiritual sloth. It deeply saddens me when in the House of God African-American christians reject the Word of God concerning their spiritual legacy and the prophetic place we occupy in Scripture. Many of these brothers and sisters grin and shuffle their feet, shout hallelujah for unity in the body while their own children struggle for identity and meaning. This is foolish and hypocritical. God is calling an aggressive people, a militant people, a people whose insistence upon complete human dignity is uncompromising. Dignity for Alkebu-lan and her disbursed children, dignity for our Spanish, Asian, Ta-Nehisi (Ethiopian) Jewish and also our European brothers and sisters.

It is our European brothers and sisters who must confront the ignominy of their history. They must face the shame of plagiarism and the falsification of history. They must acknowledge the spiritual and psychological warfare of Western Europeanized "knowledge" institutions and political policies. Our European brothers must join us in our search for truth. When they discover truth they must preach it from their pulpits and over the radio and television waves. They must risk their popularity, their financial support and every thing they have which is built upon the approach of taking the low road. Foolish notions that increased church attendance and revival are synonymous must give way to careful research into the history of revivals and their contemporary social settings. Preachers must abandon soft preaching and shallow program oriented Christianity in favor of the prophetic message of Jesus concerning the Kingdom of God. Our white brothers who ignore the conditions of America's poor and disenfranchised must stand with us in a solid front decrying government established ghetcolonies in America and the Third World. The love we speak of cannot be that of disengagement and demagoguery. I John 3:18 says, "Dear children, let us not love with words or tongue but with actions and in truth." "Seeking refuge behind a superficial and private philanthropy will not appease God who calls for justice, mercy, and truth" (Matthew 23:23).

To exclude our white (European brothers) in the name of Nationalism is to make it too easy for them; and is reactionary, nonproductive, and ultimately sinful for us. No, truth which reveals the universality of injustice and the responsibility of discipleship refuses to accept easy excuses. No, this issue of racism at each moment is the responsibility of every believer. I love my brothers too much to allow them to lapse into irresponsibility of the magnitude which ultimately denies the faith.

We are not asking our white brothers to don dashikis, and African medallions. We are not asking them to affect black language and cultural styles. We are asking for an openness to truth and a commitment to radical Christian discipleship from the entire Body of Christ. Micah 6:8 is clearly a prophetic call to a depth of belief and action. The prophet is told by God, "He has showed you, O man, what is good. And what does the Lord require of you. To act justly and to love mercy and to walk humbly with your God." No believer in God, Christ, and the Holy Spirit has a right Biblically to stand idly while injustice dehumanizes and destroys throngs of people. Now because of our commitment to Biblical reconciliation we will stand with our

European brothers and sisters all the way through this process. We will stand however, thoroughly purged of fear, subservience, and an unwillingness to lead them and our own people to the cross of Christ for true reconciliation and to the resurrection for transformation.

Children of Alkebu-lan(the African-American segment of the Body) we must not abuse "The Light." The Light must illuminate our minds and spirits and put us on a path toward repentance, restoration and renewal. For then an only then shall we be allowed to call ourselves the Church of the Living God. For then and only then will the Church have anything but a neglible, comprised and shallow impact on the systems of this world.

Children of Alkebu-lan our anger must be constructive (Ephesians 4:26; Ecclesiastes 7:9). We must control our anger and allow it to propel us forward with a fresh vision and burning conviction to see Satan toppled. The poison of hatred must not enter our hearts, and the dainty meats of arrogance must not immobilize our strageties. Armed with the faith of our forefathers the prophets, we will not give in to despair. We will continue to look to the hills from whence cometh our help and we will insist upon radical prohetic love which is often forged in the crucible of confessed pain and mistrust purified by the flames of faith and hope.

Proverbs 31:8-9 says, "Speak up for those who cannot speak for themselves, for the rights of all who are destitute. Speak up and judge fairly; defend the right of the poor and needy." (NIV)

FOUR

Blacks and Biblical Covenant

Every single covenant that God has made with man has involved Africans. Though the Bible never refers to any such group (Africans) there are several other Hebrew and Greek terms which refer to the land and inhabitants of Alkebu-lan (Africa).

Africans were involved in the so-called Adamic Covenant inasmuch as Adam themselves was African. (Genesis 1:27) We see again Africans or Blacks in the Noahic Covenant. In Genesis 10 where the Table of Nations is found there are no less than twenty five African names mentioned directly or by descendants. Cush was Noah's grandson and as has already been stated, Cush means Black or Black-skinned.

In the Mosiac Covenant we find Moses taking an Ethiopian (Ta-Nehisi or Black faced) wife. Her name was Zipporah. Black Zipporah bore Moses two sons, Gershom and Eliezer. Zipporah was the daughter of godly Jethro (Raguel: Numbers 10:29). Moses sought the counsel and blessing of Jethro. Exodus 4:18 says, "Moses went and returned to Jethro his father-in-law, and said unto him, Let me go I pray thee, and return unto my brethren, which are in Egypt, and see whether they be yet alive. And Jethro said

39

to Moses, Go in peace." Peace here in this verse is the word Shalom. Shalom or Shalam means to be safe; it means wealth, prosperity, to have whole welfare, to be favored; it means to be completed, to be finished or made fully properous. Shalom is a covenant term and Black Jethro used it to bless Moses. We know that Moses ultimately prospers on this journey so Jethro was used of the Lord to confirm the Word of the Lord, and the Lord's purpose and direction for Moses' life and ministry.

It was Zipporah however, who saved Moses' life and ministry. When Moses was equivocating with God by not circumcising their child thusly not ordaining even all his family to the purposes of God and leaving himself an out, Zipporah discerned the Lord's purpose.

Exodus 4:24-26 says, "And it came to pass by the way in the inn, that the Lord met him, (Moses) and sought to kill him. Then Zipporah took a sharp stone and cut off the foreskin of the flesh of her son and cast it at his feet, and said, Surely a bloody husband art thou to me. So He let him go; then she said, A bloody husband thou art, because of the circumcision."

We must become so enthralled with the Lord's purposes that we sow our families into the same covenant of purpose and ministry. For not to do this can surely only bring death. Thank God for the spiritual sensitivity of Zipporah. I should note here that both Moses and Zipporah would have been familiar with circumcision inasmuch as it was an ancient Egyptian practice.

The so-called Abrahamic Covenant was not without African involvement. Genesis 16:1 says, "Now Sarai Abram's wife bore him no children: and she had a handmaiden, an Egyptian whose name was Hagar." Verse four says, "And he (Abram) went unto Hagar and she conceived...." Now look at verse eleven: "And the angel of the Lord said unto her, (Egyptian Hagar) Behold, thou art with child, and shalt bear a son, and shalt call him Ishmael;

40

because the Lord hath heard thy affliction." We must note that though the actual covenant through Abraham was with Isaac, Ishmael still did receive the blessing of Genesis 12:1-3 (Genesis 17:20). The children of Ishmael are the Arabs. The selection of Isaac as the child of promise had absolutely nothing to do with skin color, Abraham himself being from Ur of the Black Chaldeans.

Then there is the Noahic Covenant. Genesis 9:18-19 says, "And the sons of Noah, that went forth of the ark, were Shem, and Ham, and Japheth: and Ham is the father of Canaan. These are the three sons of Noah: and of them was the whole earth overspread." Now over in Genesis 10 we see the generations of Noah through his son Ham. Genesis 10:6-20 tells us who the sons of Ham were. It was out of the loins of Ham that the great African (Alkebu-lan) nations of Cush (Kush, Ethiopia) and Mizraim (Egypt, Ta-Merry) came. We also see that several other nations came out of the loins of Black Ham.

God is a God of generations and nations. It is time that we begin to teach our young men and women that God wants to raise up generations and nations through their loins. God's promise to Adam was one of generations and nations. God's promise to Abraham was one of generations and nations. God's promise to Moses was one of a nation, God's promise to Noah was that of a new people, a nation, and finally God's promise through Jesus is one of a chosen priesthood and a royal nation.

Africans were also involved in the Davidic Covenant. Not long after God had given the Word of the Lord to David through Nathan the Prophet concerning a house, a kingdom and a throne eternally established (II Samuel 7:16) something cataclysmic occured. II Samuel 11:2-5 says: "And it came to pass in an eveningtide that David arose from off his bed, and walked upon the roof of the king's house: and from the roof he saw a woman washing herself; and the woman was very beautiful to look upon.

41

And David sent and inquired after the woman. And one said, Is not this Bath-sheba, the daughter of Eliam, the wife of Uriah the Hittite? And David sent messengers, and took her; and came in unto him, and he lay with her; for she was purified from her uncleanness: she returned unto her house; And the woman conceived and sent and told David, and said, I am with child."

You know the rest of the story, sin's vicious cycle began spinning. David had Bath-sheba's husband Uriah the Hittite sent to the front lines of military engagement therely insuring his death. David then married Bath-sheba and she bore him a son. However, II Samuel 12:15-23 tells us that the child died. This was not the end. Bath-sheba, whose name means daughter of Sheba (blackskinned, Genesis 10:7), bore David another son. II Samuel 12:24-25 says: "And David comforted Bath-sheba his wife, and went in unto her, and lay with her: and she bore a son, and he called his name Solomon: and the Lord loved him. And he sent by the hand of Nathan the prophet; and he called his name Jedidiah, because of the Lord." Jedidiah means "Beloved of Jah," "Jah" is Jehovah. Jedidiah also means "a love token," a friend, to boil. Jehovah had a boiling loving friendship toward Solomon (Jedidiah).

It is not without significance that Solomon's name means "beloved of Jah" or "beloved of Jehovah" as opposed to "beloved of Elohim." Between Genesis 1:1 and 2:4 the name "Elohim" occurs thirty five times. "Elohim" by His great and mighty power creates, governs and sustains the cosmos. "Elohim" denotes omnipotence and sovereignty. "Jah" or "Jehovah" on the other hand are derived from the Hebrew verb chavah, which means "to live or have life." It denotes the eternity and unchangeableness of God. Psalm 102:27 says: "But thou art the same, and thy years shall have no end."

Jehovah is the name of God used to impart revelation. Exodus 3:13-15 says: "And Moses said unto God, Behold, when I come unto the children of Israel, and shall say unto them, The God of your fathers hath sent me, What is his name? What shall I say unto them? And God said unto Moses I AM THAT I AM hath sent you. And God said moreover unto Moses, Thus shalt thou say unto the children of Israel, The Lord God of your fathers, the God of Abraham, the God of Isaac, and the God of Jacob, hath sent me unto you: this is my name forever, and this is my memorial unto all generations."

In Exodus 3:14 the word AM is "havah" which in Hebrew means breath. It is also the word "avah" which means to wish, long desire, lust after or covet. Finally, it is the word "hayah" which means to exist, become, or altogether come to pass: it also means "committed to accomplishing."

God, Jehovah, the revealing, covenant making, never covenant breaking God wants to do more than give us goose pimples and make us shout. Don't get me wrong, I love to shout and praise God. This is the hour, though when God wants to reveal Himself to us as I AM. Jehovah did reveal Himself to Solomon (Jedidiah) and tremendous things happened in Solomon's life. God wants to do tremendous, stupefying, awe-inspiring, history making, earth shaking things in our lives, but we must first allow Him to reveal Himself to us. We must begin to hunger and thirst after righteousness. The Father is in this hour going to so saturate the minds of His children with His plan, His purpose and His wisdom that the minds of men will be flabbergasted. Please be patient with me in belaboring Solomon (Jedidiah), there is much to be gained by type and shadow from him.

Africans were also involved in covenant with Joseph, and this is very significant. Genesis 41:45 says, "And Pharoah called Joseph's name Zaphnath-paaneah; and he gave him to wife Asenath the daughter of Potipherah priest of On. And Joseph went out over all the land of

Egypt."

On, which means strength, was an Egyptian city. In Jeremiah 43:13 the prophet refers to On as "Beth-shemesh, that is in the land of Egypt. Situated ten miles N.E. of modern Cairo it was the same as Heliopolis which was the chief city of Egyptian science and one of four great cities Herodotus speaks of as being noted for religious festivals in honor of the sun.

Joseph and Egyptian (Black) Asenath bore two sons. Genesis 41:50-52 says, "And unto Joseph were born two sons before the years of famine came, which Asenath the daughter of Potipherah priest of On bore unto him. And Joseph called the name of the firstborn Manasseh: For God, said he hath made me forget all my toil, and all my father's house. And the name of the second he called Ephraim: For God hath caused me to be fruitful in the land of my affliction."

Genesis 46:20 says, "And unto Joseph in the land of Egypt were born Manasseh and Ephraim, which Asenath the daughter of Potipherah priest of On bore unto him."

Now let us move ahead and get a glimpse into the destiny of these two young Black males. Genesis 48:1-5 says, "And it came to pass after these things, that one told Joseph, behold, thy father is sick: and he took with him his two sons, Manasseh and Ephraim. And one told Jacob, and said, Behold thy son Joseph cometh unto thee: and Israel strengthened himself and sat upon the bed, And Jacob said unto Joseph, God Almighty appeared unto me at Luz (Canaanite name of Beth-el) in the land of Canaan, and blessed me, And said unto me, Behold, I will make thee fruitful, and multiply thee, and I will make of thee a multitude of people: and will give this land to thy seed after thee for an everlasting possession. And now thy two sons, Ephraim and Manasseh, which were born unto thee in the land of Egypt, before I came unto thee into Egypt, are mine: as Rueben and Simeon, they shall be mine."

Then comes a very tender moment in the life of this family. Three generations of men gather and something powerful happens. Let us examine Genesis 48:8-22. It reads, "And Israel beheld Joseph's sons, and said, Who are these? And Joseph said unto his father, They are my sons, whom God hath given me in this place. And he said, Bring them, I pray thee, unto me and I will bless them. Now the eyes of Israel were dim for age, so that he could not see. And he brought them near unto him; and he kissed them, and embraced them. And Israel said unto Joseph, I had not thought to see thy face; and lo, God hath shown me also thy seed. And Joseph brought them out from between his knees, and he bowed himself with his face to the earth. And Joseph took them both, Ephraim in his right hand toward Israel's left hand, and Manasseh in his left hand toward Israel's right hand, and brought them near unto him. And Israel stretched out his right hand, and laid it upon Ephraim's head, who was the younger, and his left hand upon Manasseh's head, guiding his hand wittingly; for Manasseh was the firstborn. And he blessed Joseph, and said God, before whom my fathers Abraham and Isaac did walk, the God which fed me all my life long unto this day. The angel which redeemed me from all evil, bless the lads; and let my name be named on thence, and the name of my fathers Abraham and Isaac; and let them grow into multitudes in the midst of the earth. And when Joseph saw that his father laid his right hand upon the head of Ephraim, it displeased him: and he held up his father's hand, to remove it from Ephraim's head unto Manasseh's head. And Joseph said unto his father, Not so, my father: for this is the firstborn: put thy right hand upon his head. And his father refused, and said, I know it, my son, I know it; he also shall become a people, and he also shall be great: but truly his younger brother shall be greater that he, and his seed shall become a multitude of nations. And he blessed them that day, saying, In thee shall Israel bless, saying, God make thee as Ephraim and as Manasseh: and he set Ephraim before Manasseh. And Israel said unto Joseph, Behold I die; but God shall be with you, and bring you again unto the land of your fathers. Moreover, I have given to thee one portion above thy brethren, which I took out of the hand of the Amorite with my sword and bow."

In an hour of crumbling African-American families this story inspires hope. The patriarch who has given up on ever seeing his son again not only gets to see and bless his son but also his grandsons. A strong, godly, and powerful grandfather prophesying and imparting blessing and destiny to his black progeny. Jacob (Israel) decreed the blessing of Abraham and Isaac over Black Manasseh and Ephraim. There is both a natural and a spiritual application of this blessing.

In Genesis 12 God promises Abraham some profound things. Genesis 12:2-3 says, "And I will make of thee a great nation, and I will bless thee, and make thy name great; and thou shalt be a blessing. And I will bless them that bless thee, and curse him that curseth thee: and in thee shall all families of the earth be blessed."

One need not wonder whether God honors His word. Abraham obeyed God and departed from Ur of the Black Chaldeans into Black Egypt (Ta-Merry) not knowing clearly what the future held. Abraham's faith was his guide. Now let us see the power of God to conceive, birth, and honor His purpose combined with our faith. Genesis 12:10 says: "And there was a famine in the land: and Abram went down into Egypt to sojourn there; for the famine was grievous in the land. The word grievous is from the Hebrew kabed (kaw-bade). It means heavy, severe, so great, hardened, too heavy, slow, sore thick, or stupid. It was into this land where God sent Abraham, he went into stupid, too heavy, great famine. However, God's purpose for his life did not end there. How did Abraham come out of this Egyptian famine? Genesis 13:1-2 says:

"And Abram went up out of Egypt, he and his wife, and all that he had, and Lot with him, into the south. And Abram was very rich in cattle, in silver, and in gold." The word rich is from a Hebrew word which means numerous, honorable, abounding, glorious, to make weighty. This was Abraham's blessing, a nation, a family, all families, honor, wealth, faith, a very blessed seed. God also anointed Abraham as a prophet. (See Genesis 20:7)

I need to further say that through covenant blessing in Genesis 17:7,8 God gives unto Abraham "all the land of (Black) Canaan, for can everlasting possession..."

Later Abraham's senior servant saddled up the dromedaries and went into Black Mesopotamia to find Master Isaac a wife. When he found Rebekah, he testified to her father concerning Abraham. Genesis 24:34,36,38 says' "And he said, I am Abraham's servant. And the Lord hath blessed my master greatly, and he is become great: and he hath given him flocks, and herds, and silver, and gold, and manservants, and maidservants, and camels, and asses. And Sarah my master's wife bore a son to my master when she was old: and unto him hath he given all that he hath. Abraham had to obey the Word of God. Proverbs 13:22 says, "A good man leaveth an inheritance to his children's children: and the wealth of the sinner is laid up for the just." Both portions of this scripture verse are fulfilled in the Abraham, Isaac covenant.

Now brothers if you really want to win that godly, gorgeous sister. If you want to covenant with her this is how you do it. Send your servant to her in this fashion. Genesis 24:53 says, "And the servant brought forth jewels of silver, and jewels of gold, and raiment, and gave them to Rebekah: he gave also to her brother and to her mother precious things." Abraham and Isaac were sealed into this family. Notice that God did not descend upon Mesopotamia, rebuke the servant for boasting of His blessing upon Abraham and then thrash Abraham for poor stewardship.

No, Hallelujah, Jehovah God enjoyed every moment of this.

Favor was gained through blessing. This will eliminate mother-in-law woes forever. In fact as Rebekah was leaving her family her mother said, "Thou art our sister, be thou the mother of thousands and millions, and let thy seed possess the gate of those which hate them." In so decreeing Rebekah's family released her to be joined to Isaac's prophetic and generational covenant, of purpose, destiny and prosperity.

In the American family marriage ceremony the preacher may ever so piously have you to rejoin "for richer or for poorer," that may sound good and religious but it certainly is not Biblical.

This is but a glimpse of Abraham and Isaac's blessing which Jacob received and conferred upon Manasseh and Ephraim. Both of Joseph's sons became ancestors of tribes of Israel which bore their respective names. These were two explicitly Black tribes.

As the seed of Abraham this blessing of covenant, nation, family, seed prosperity, and honor is yours. However, Satan does not want you to have it. But I repeat it is yours and you must take back what is yours.

African involvement in Biblical covenants and with key Biblical characters does not end with David. I Kings 3:1 says: "And Solomon had affinity with Pharoah king of Egypt, and took Pharoah's daughter, and brought her into the city of David, until he had made an end of building his own house, and the house of the Lord, and the wall of Jerusalem round about." Affinity is the Hebrew word chathan (khaw-than). It means a contract, or to give away in marriage. The Ta-Merrian (Black Egyptian) daughter of Pharoah was the First Lady (Queen) of Jerusalem.

This black woman is spoken of in Songs of Solomon 1:5. Before I comment on the verse I should like to remind you, particularly Black, Spanish and Asian students of the

Bible of the Conspiracy Against Color on the part of many major European and Euro-American interpreters, exegetis and commentators. Do not be deceived by twisted language, insertions (e.g. King James Version) and/or inuendo. Study to show yourselves approved.

In Songs 1:5 the Pharoah's daughter is not ashamed of her Blackness as it would appear upon a shallow reading of the text. She says: "I am black, but comely, Oh ye daughters of Jerusalem, as the tents of Kedar, as the curtains of Solomons." This Black daughter of a Ta-Merrian (Egyptian) Pharoah describes herself as comely. "Comely" is from the Hebrew word naah or naneh. It means beautiful, suitable; it also means to be at home or a lovely dwelling. This sister was at home with her own beauty, she was pleasant in personality, and also right at home by Solomon, the King of Israel and Judah. In fact "but" is not found in original manuscripts. This Egyptian Princess declares herself "black **and** beautiful."

I Kings 3:5 says, "In Gibeon the Lord appeared to Solomon in a dream by night; and God said, Ask what I shall give thee." Solomon responds in I Kings 3:8-9. "And thy servant is in the midst of thy people which thou hast chosen, a great people, that cannot be numbered nor counted for the multitude. Give therefore thy servant an understanding heart to judge thy people, that I may discern between good and bad: for who is able to judge this thy so great a people? Now let us note God's (Jehovah) response to Solomon in I Kings 3:10-14 "And the speech pleased the Lord, that Solomon had asked this thing. And God said unto him, Because thou hast asked this thing, and hast not asked for thyself long life: neither hast asked riches for thyself, nor hast asked the life of thine enemies; but hast asked for thyself understanding to discern judgement; Behold, I have done according to thy word: lo, I have given thee a wise and understanding heart; so that there was none like thee before thee, neither after thee shall arise any like unto thee. And I have also given thee that which thou has not asked, both riches and honour: so that there shall not be any among the kings like unto thee all thy days. And if thou wilt walk in my ways, to keep my statutes and my commandments, as thy father David did walk, then I will lengthen thy days."

I Kings 3:15 is very important to all of this! "And Solomon awoke; and, behold it was a dream. And he came to Jerusalem, and stood before the ark of the covenant of the Lord, and offered up burnt offerings, and offered peace offerings, and made a feast to all his servants." Solomon dreamt all of this yet every jot and tittle came to pass. What has God spoken to you in a dream or vision. Dreams and visions are as Paul Yongi Cho would say, "the language of the Holy Spirit." Joel 2:28 says: "...I will pour out my Spirit upon all flesh; and you sons and daughters shall prophesy, your old men shall dream dreams, your young men shall see visions..."

Dreams and visions are two of the ways the Lord uses to reveal purpose and destiny for our lives. *Do Not Ignore Your Dreams and Visions.* Had Solomon ignored his dream he would have missed his purpose and forfeited his destiny. When you have a dream or a vision take it to the Apostles, Prophets, Bishops and Elders in the "House" where you are planted. The Presbytery is able to confirm God's purpose for your life (I Timothy 4:14). Your dreams and visions then become "spiritual" weapons used to pull down strongholds of defeat, purposelessness and inferiority. (II Corinthians 10:2-7)

Before we move on to look at the Queen of Sheba I would like to make one last comment directly concerning Solomon. Solomon's mother, Black beautiful Bath-sheba, was involved in securing a kingly destiny for her son. I Kings 1:16-17 says: "And Bath-sheba bowed, and did obeisance unto the king. And the king said, What wouldest thou? And she said unto him, My lord, thou swarest by the Lord thy God unto thine handmaid, saying, Assuredly Solomon thy son shall reign after me, and he shall sit upon my throne." David's response is found in I Kings 1:28-30 "Then king David answered and said, Call me Bath-sheba. And she came into the king's presence, and stood before the king. And the king swore, and said, As the Lord liveth, that hath redeemed my soul out of all distress. Even as I swore unto thee by the Lord God of Israel, saying, Assuredly Solomon thy son shall reign after me, and he shall sit upon my throne in my stead; even so will I certainly do this day."

Mothers and Fathers I exhort and implore you in Jesus' name. Get into agreement on behalf of the children. Dare to be as bold as Bath-sheba. Pray that our children reign in the things of God. Pray that they reign in wisdom, science, in art, in politics, diplomacy, in finance, in business and commerce, in marriage and family, in loyalty and integrity. Pray that they become writers, film makers, producers, animators, congress persons, judges, lawyers, teachers, scientists, professors, apostles, prophets, diplomats and leaders all to the Glory of God! Pray that they move in great sensitivity to the precious Holy Spirit and allow Him to manifest Himself in and through them!

FIVE

Africa's Legacy of Prosperity

"And when the Queen of Sheba heard of the fame of Solomon concerning the name of the Lord, she came to prove him with hard questions. And she came to Jerusalem with a very great train, with camels that bore spices, and very much gold, and precious stones: and when she was come to Solomon, she communed with him all that was in her heart."

Her name was Makeda or Bilkis. She was Black, beautiful, and royal. She was from a dynasty which had been founded by Za Besi Angabo around 1370 B.C.E. in Ethiopia. She and her train of almost eight hundred camels and donkeys had travelled 1250 miles carrying an impressive array of riches. Makeda was accompanied by almost two hundred highly trained palace guardsmen as well as philosophers, cartographers, jewelers, priests, leather workers, chemists, etc. In command of this royal caravan under Makeda was Tamrin. Tamrin was a skilled tradesman and a well-travelled gentleman whose reputation for astuteness preceeded him. All told the queen's booty of gold, spices, and precious stone is believed to have been worth more than twenty five million dollars.

Makeda, the Queen of Sheba, is also mentioned in II

Chronicles 9:1-12. Sheba in addition to being mentioned in the Tables of Nations, (Genesis 10) is also mentioned in Isaiah 43:3; 60:6; Ezekiel 27:22-23; Jeremiah 6:20; and Psalm 72:10 which says: "The kings of Tarshish and of the isles shall bring presents: the kings of Sheba and Seba shall offer gifts."

I need to comment on the latter clause of Psalm 71:10 "...the kings of Sheba and Seba shall offer gifts." The African and African-American segments of the Body of Christ along with specifically our Spanish and Spanish-American brothers and sisters are the king (and queens) of Sheba and Seba. In the Table of Nations (Genesis 10) Seba was the son of Cush (Kush, Ethio-Eburut) ops (face) and Sheba was the grandson of Cush. This makes both Sheba and Seba Black nations.

The word "offer" in Psa. 72:10 is the Hebrew word garab (kaw-rab). It means to approach, to make ready, to be at hand, to draw near. To draw near and offer gifts. Over the past two decades with the teaching on faith, healing, and prosperity there has been conspicious absences of ethnic teachers, writers, televisers. Do not misunderstand. The writing, television ministries of Kenneth E. Hagin, Kenneth Copeland, Jerry Savelle, Dr. Oral and Richard Roberts, and Casey Treat lifted the veil of tradition and denominationalism from my eyes and allowed me to see that God is a now God. I have been blessed by these great men of God.

However, as I browsed Christian book stores, subscribed to Christian magazines, viewed Christian television, and listened to Christian radio I wondered why there were not more of Dr. Frederick K. C. Price and Carlton Pearsons. Now as I look at the horizon by the Spirit I see Dr. Myles Munroe, Dr. Bernard Jordan, Tony Morris, Jeff Edwards, Dr. Leonard Lucas, Clifford Turner and others bringing gifts.

Some may ask why this is important. As has been

noted by Jefferson Edwards in "Chosen Not Cursed" there has been no major move of God among the African-American segment of the Body of Christ since Azusa Street in 1906. If one surveys the Christian landscape one finds that Christianity generated fifty billion dollars in America in 1989. However, most publishing houses, television stations, Christian retail businesses, colleges and universities are owned or controlled by our European and Euro-American brothers and sisters. This is not good. Proverbs 13:22 says, "A good man leaveth an inheritiance to his children's children: and the wealth of the sinner is laid up for the just." If we as Black and Brown Christians own no wealth, how may we leave any inheritance to anyone?

We, in the African-American segment of the Body of Christ must become wise and astute. We must do more than cry and dance in our churches. Please hear my heart. The last thing on earth I intend to do is ridicule someone's emotional and Christ-centered experience of worship. However, I hear the voice of the Spirit crying for more. The Holy Spirit is yearning to make us a witness in the world. Hear the Word of the Lord concerning wisdom. Proverbs 3:16 says, "Length of days is in her (wisdom's) right hand and in her left hand riches and honor."

The Church of the living God is the answer to the blight being suffered by the inner cities of America. We have given to us in the Biblical practical guidelines, principles for living life sucessfully. I believe that the life giving principles spoken by Jehovah, the revealing, covenant making God give purpose to lives being destroyed by all manner of satanic strategies.

Much is said in the Bible concerning the wealth of Alkebu-lan (Africa). Again speaking of wisdom and searching for a point of reference to its value Job says in chapter twenty-eight, verse nineteen, "The topaz of Ethiopia shall not equal it, neither shall it be valued with pure gold." Genesis 2:11-12 says: "The name of the first (river) is Pison: that is it which compasseth the whole land of Havilah where there is gold; and the gold of that land is good: there is bdelluim and onyx stone." Bdelluim is the ruby stone with its brilliant red color."

In I Chronicles chapter twenty nine, David has prepared an offering for the Temple of Solomon. In David's offering was gold from Ophir. Look at I Chronicles 29:4, "Even three thousand talents of gold, of the gold, of Ophir...."

Job 22:21-24 says: "Acquaint now thyself with him and be at peace: thereby good shall come unto thee. Receive, I pray thee, the law from his mouth, and lay up his words in thy ear. If thou return to the Almighty, thou shalt be built up, thou shalt put away iniquity far from thy tabernacles. Then shalt thou lay up gold as dust, and the gold of Ophir as the stones of the brooks."

W. E. B. DuBois wrote of the gold of Ophir, "Beyond Ethiopia, in Central and South Africa, lay the gold of Ophir and the rich trade of Punt on which the prosperity of Egypt largely depended." (DuBois, 1946,1990)

There is another beautiful passage referring to Ophir's gold. Psalm 45:6-9 says: "Thy throne, O God, is for ever and ever: the sceptre of thy kingdom is a right sceptre. Thou lovest righteousness, and hatest wickedness: therefore God, thy God, both anointed thee with the oil of gladness above thy fellows. All thy garments smell of myrrh, and aloes, and cassia, out of the ivory palaces, whereby they have made thee glad. King's daughters were among thy honourable women: upon thy right hand did stand the queen in gold of Ophir.

Solomon's building projects were largely supplied with materials from Africa. I Kings 9:11 says: "Now Hiram the King of Tyre had furnished Solomon with cedar trees and fir trees, and with gold, according to all his desire, that then King Solomon have Hiram twenty cities in the land of Galilee." Tyre was a city founded by the Phoenicians. The Phoenicians were great merchants and mariners.

They were the manufacturers of a valuable and famous dye known as "royal purple." The Greeks called this dye Phoenixes and thus nicknamed these east Africans from Punt, Phoenicians. It was the Phoenicians who colonized much of the western Mediterranean coast and established Carthage (Khart-Haddas, The New Town) on the African coast in 814 B.C.E. The Carthagenians (Khart-Haddans) established other colonies along the coast of Northern Africa, Northwestern Africa, and Southeastern Spain.

Carthage (Khart-Haddas) this city founded by Black Phoenicians became a world power. In 509 Carthage signed a Treaty of Friendship with Rome and in 500 set up an embassy in that great city. It was during this period that Carthage (Khart-Haddas) and Rome were the most feared and respected cities in Africa (Alkebu-lan) and Europe respectively.

Though another volume could be written on the history of Carthage (Khart-Haddas) and Rome, a few more historical comments will have to suffice. Around 600 B.C.E. when Khart-Haddas had established trading posts in Southeastern Spain she seized Spain's silver mines. She then proceeded to seize Spain's tin trade with Britain as well as control of the Strait of Gibraltar. It is this history between Africa and Europe's strongest cities that give rise to the greatest military general the world has known, General Hannibal Barca. Between c. 216-214 B.C.E. General Hannibal Barca destroyed three Roman armies in the so-called Punic wars. Over the course of several valiantly fought, strategically imitable campaigns Carthage was ultimately defeated. In 146 B.C.E. Rome set fire to the great city.

It may seem as though I am belaboring the point of Africa's gold and riches, but the point warrants belaboring. The so-called "Great Western Empires" have all built their economic infrastructures with wealth stolen from Alkebu-lan and her children. The late Guyanese scholar/activist Walter Rodney in "How Europe Under-developed Africa" wrote: "Europeans were anxious to acquire gold in Africa because there was a pressing need for gold coin within the growing capitalist economy. We all know that it was not only gold but slave labor from Africa which financed and built the Western Empires. Rodney further states: "In speaking of the Europeans slave trade, mention must be made of the U.S.A., not only because its dominant population was European but also because Europe transferred its capitalist institutions more completely to North America than to any other part of the globe, and established a powerful form of capitalism-after eliminating the indigenous inhabitants and exploiting the labor of millions of Africans." (Rodney, 1972)

In addition to allowing Europe and later America to monopolize transnational trade, wealth stolen from Africa also funded scientific research, and strengthened European military forces.

The poverty, joblessness, family fragmentation, urban despair and rampant nihilism affecting so much of America's and the world's Black population is abnormal. The inner cities of America are crying out for a prophetic church, the church in the spirit of Jesus Christ. The church that will give birth to a vision for the transformation of urban America. The Church all over America must redefine its mission statement. Self righteous holier than thouism or escapism will not address the malignant spiritual problems of America. No one can be written off, not gang members nor drug dealers, not crack mothers nor school drop-outs or worst still those who seem to have abandoned hope and given up. It was precisely to those marginalized ones that Jesus came.

Luke 4:18-19 says, "The spirit of the Lord is upon me; he has appointed me to preach Good News to the poor; he has sent me to heal the broken-hearted and to announce that captives shall be released and the blind shall see, that downtrodden shall be freed from their oppressors, and that God is ready to give blessings to all who come to him." Poverty, despair, urban nihilism, and fragmented families, these are spiritual issues. There is no group of people upon the earth who have poverty as a "Divine Desire" of God.

W. E. B. DuBois published "The World and Africa" in 1946. A more recent edition of that work was published in 1965 into fresh material which Dr. DuBois had written between 1955-1961. Dr. DuBois wrote a series of articles for the National Guardian between February and April 1955. In the article "The Giant Stir" this eminent African-American scholar wrote: "Today out of Africa come 95 percent of the world's diamonds; 80 percent of the cobalt; 60 percent of the gold; 75 percent of the sesal hemp; 70 percent of the palm oil; 70 percent of the cocoa; 35 percent of the phosphates; 30 percent of the chrome and manganese; 20 percent of the copper; 15 percent of the coffee; an increasing part of the uranium and radium, and large amount of tin, iron and spices." Dr. DuBois goes on to inform us that during the first half of the twentieth century American investment in Africa rose from $500 million to $1500 million (DuBois 1965). Think also in terms of the hundreds of millions of dollars in capitalist dollars southern whites profited as African slave labor produced tobacco and later made cotton king.

The Honorable Marcus M. Garvey stated; "Behind the murder of millions of Negroes annually in Africa is the well organized system of exploitation by the alien intruders who desire to rob Africa of every bit of its wealth for the satisfaction of their race and the upkeep of their bankrupt European countries." (Amy Jacques-Garvey; Atheneum 1986)

In "The Rising Tide of Colour" Lothrop Stoddard wrote: "...the white man has every reason for keeping a "firm hold on Africa" (p. 50 deGraft Johnson).

SIX

African Foundations
of Christianity
(Prologue)

T he more research I embark upon and the more time I
spend in reflection upon the fruit of the researches the
more cynical is my attitude toward "Christianity" becoming. Mind you, I did not say that I was becoming cynical
toward Christ or God or the Holy Spirit or the Holy
Scriptures. However, the manner in which the Western
Religio-Political, Socio-ethical, Psycho-spiritual paradigm
has deliberately distorted the image of God, the persons
of Christ and the Holy Spirit, and systematically falsified
both hermeneutics and history has left us with a spiritual,
historical, social, political, economic and cognitive waste-
land. What is needed are some Nehemiah's to accurately
survey and assess the damages and commit to rebuilding
the dwelling place of God.

Christianity has been the chief corner stone of North
America racism. In a deliciously irreverent book entitled
"The Arrogance of Faith" author Forrest G. Wood writes,
"The central thesis of this book is that Christianity in the
five centuries since its message was first carried to the
peoples of the New World-and in particular, to the natures
and the transplanted Africans of English North America
and the United States-has been fundamentally racist in its

59

ideology, organization, and practice." Christianity as racism, to the mind searching for truth this concept is oxymoronic. "Western's New World Dictionary" defines an oxymoron as "a figure of speech in which opposite or contradictory ideas or terms are combined." The literal meaning is from the Greek oxymoros which means acutely silly. One would like to think of the notion of Christianity as the chief cornerstone of racism as acutely silly, however, history strongly excludes humor from this matter and exposes the painful and absurd reality.

Every member of the Body of Christ interested in true unity must understand the history, past and present of racism. To this and I suggest that every pastor, church leader, or concerned Christian in America should read Neely Fuller's "the United Independent Compensatory Code System Concept" and Dr. Frances Cress Welsing's "The Isis Papers." On page twenty-four of Fuller's work he defines racism as "One or more white persons using deceit, direct violence and/or the threat of violence, to promote falsehood, non-justice, and/or incorrectness, against non-white people, in one or more areas of activity, including economics, education, entertainment, labor, law, politics, religion, sex and/or war." According to Fuller, racism (white supremacy) has four stages. They are as follows: 1. Establishment; 2. Maintenance; 3. Expansion; 4. Refinement. Inasmuch as "Christianity" is the foundation of a system of worldwide oppression, falsification, and dehumanization, it is evil.

Please understand my unequivocal commitment to the historic doctrine of salvation through the redemptive sacrifice of Jesus Christ. I believe however, that racism is a powerful Satanic stronghold. The word "stronghold" is found in II Corinthians 10:4. It is the Greek word *Echuroma* which means a fortress. A fortress in the Old Testament is defined by four different words. *Matsawd;* which means a castle or defense, a strong place, a castle, to be hunted, netted or snared. *Mibtsar* (mib-tsawr) means a fortified city, a defender, a castle, or fortification, a fenced, or protected place. This word is a derivative from *batsar* (baw-tsar). *Batsar* means to be isolated (inaccessible by height or fortification, a strong, restrained, mighty, walled-up thing, a place of withholding. Next there is the Hebrew word *matsowr* (maw-tsore) which implies the existence of borders, something hemmed in, beseiged places, a bullwark or tower. Finally there is the word *maoioz* (maw-oze) which means a srengthened or most strengthened stronghold. W. E. Vine adds that "stronghold" is used metaphorically in 2 Cor. 10:4, of those things in which mere human confidence is imposed."

We need to further examine II Corinthians 10:4-5. The Amplified Bible (translation) renders the two verses as follows: "For the weapons of our warfare are not physical (weapons of flesh and blood), but they are mighty before God for the overthrow and destruction of strongholds, (Inasmuch as we) refute arguments and theories and reasonings and every proud and lofty thing that sets itself up against the (true) knowledge of God; and we lead every thought and purpose away captive into the obedience of Christ, the Messiah, the Anointed One...."

Now before I make comments on these verses let us look at verse six. "Being in readiness to punish every (insubordinate for his) disobedience, when your own submission and obedience (as a church) are fully secure and complete."

It is obvious in this Corinthian or Pauline passage that the strongholds to which Paul refers are mental, philosophical, and ideological fortresses. When Satan, whom Jesus referred to as "...a liar and the father of lies" (John 8:44) lies it is not in isolation but one lie is only a component of a system or network of untruth. I John 5:19 says, "...the whole world is under the control of the evil one. W. E. Vine comments on Kosmos which is the Greek word for world in the epistle of John. He refers to kosmos (world) as "the present condition of human affairs in alienation from and opposition to God." Strongholds are lies inasmuch as they are of Satan, after all he is the "father of lies." The stronghold of racism with its Euro-American slave Christianity foundation is demonic.

Ephesians 2:2 refers to Satan as "...the ruler of the kingdom of the air, the spirit who is now at work in those who are disobedient." Air is from the Greek word *aer* which signifies the atmosphere. The word also means to breathe unconsciously. The Greek language also has another interesting word for world. It is the word *aion* (aheeolin) which means an age or particular period in time (history) marked by certain spiritual, moral, social, intellectual, cultural or economic characteristics. The Germans have two words used frequently to describe an aion or age. They are *zeitgeist* (tsit'gist) and *weltanshauung* (velt'an shou oon). Zeitgeist is defined as the general intellectual, moral, and cultural climate of an era; the spirit of an age. Weltanschauung is defined by Webster as "a comprehensive, esp. personal, philosophy or conception of the universe and of human life. The latter word literally means word view. *Weltanschauung* is very closely akin to the Biblical understanding of "stronghold," however, I believe that there is another term from both science and philosophy which embodies the concept of *weltanschauung* but even more closely is akin to our understanding of "stronghold." That word is paradigm.

Webster simply defines a paradigm as "a pattern, example, or model; an overall concept accepted by most people in an intellectual community, as a science, because of its effectiveness in explaining a complex process, idea, or set of data." You will notice the absence of a truth value relative to Webster's definition of a paradigm. In other words the paradigm, the set of ideas, assumptions, and beliefs held by the paradigm's constituents is not necessarily true. Its value is that it explains things. Explanations are not necessarily true or false, they are simply explanations. Since the basic definition of a paradigm includes not truth claims the entire explanation and premise(s) of the paradigm can conceivably be false, i.e. paradigms do lie. However, paradigms by virtue of their existence given the faith so-called "modern" man has in science are truth claims themselves, even if only relatively speaking. The truth claim needs however, the faith of lay person in the so-called scientist or experts professional acumen and moral stature. The scientist experiments and tells us the conclusion. He began the experiment, however, with a set of presuppositions which possibly caused him to desire a certain outcome. The presuppositions and desired outcomes fit into the larger framework of the scientist's beliefs. Regarding paradigms and scientific research the German Catholic theologian Hans Küng has written, "Normal scientific research is not very concerned to produce anything radically new but is more inclined to suppress novelties."

We must understand that a *zeitgeist*, a *weltanschauung*, a paradigm, a stronghold is often supported not only by dubious but often absolutely false science. An entire culture is built around the paradigm. This culture consists principally of the paradigm's arthitects and chief expositors. Then it consists of its own pedagogues or teachers, writers, philanthropists, and practitioners. Of course paradigms influence all nine areas of Neely Fuller's people activities: economics, education, entertainment, labor, law, politics, religion, sex, and war. The paradigms skillfully use propaganda to sell themselves.

The French sociologist Jacques Ellul in his book "Propaganda," wrote: "Most people are easy prey for propaganda because of their firm but entirely erroneous conviction that it is composed only of lies and 'tall stories' and that, conversely, what is true cannot be propaganda."

Please re-read the former statement. Ellul defines propaganda as "...the expression of opinions or actions carried out deliberately by individuals or groups with a view to influencing the opinions or actions of other individuals or group, for predetermined ends and through psychological manipulations." Finally Ellul states that propaganda embraces: 1. Psychological Action; 2. Psychological Warfare; 3. Re-education and Brainwashing; and 4. Public and Human Relations.

History offers a chilling reminder of the importance of propaganda to paradigms. In Adolf Hitler's inner circle of nineteen, one of the most important of his thugs was Paul Joseph Goebbels. In 1928 Hitler appointed Goebbels Reich Propaganda Leader for the Nazi Party. When the Nazi's assumed power in 1933, Goebbels was made Minister for Public Enlightenment and Propaganda. On June 30, 1933 a decree was issued which made Goebbels "responsible for all factors influencing the mental life of the nation, for winning allegiance to the State, its culture and its economy, for the conduct of internal and external publicity, and for the administration of all institutions contributory to those ends. As a result of this magnanimously powerful post Louis L. Snyder in "Hitler's Elite" wrote, "Goebbels now has a post of tremendous power, by which he became the de facto ruler of press, radio, cinema, theater, and virtually all cultural, scientific, and musical activities." As a government appointed propagandist Goebbels was not interested in objective truth as such, but only in advancing Nazi ideology and crushing all its opponents. Paradigms and propaganda teach people how to think, speak, write, socially interract, and also how to interpret the general political, economic and religious climate of the age.

I have belabored the similarities between the *zeitgeist*, the *weltanschauung*, and the paradigm with the need on behalf of each for propaganda all leading to my fundamental conviction regarding Christianity as practiced within and exported from the west or so-called First World. This so-called Christianity with its historical falsification, shallow ceremony and ritual, trite often vacuous messages, glamor, glitz, and hype, is a farce. It pitifully distances itself from Biblical faith, eschews prophecy, and peddles cheap grace. A so-called Christianity which has either falsified or completely denied the Africanity of its own scriptures, displaces entire populations, randomly confuses geographic locations and separates peoples and continents is at best suspect and at worst completely blasphemes. We must in fairness cite the long tradition of oppositional Christianity in the U.S. This prophetic tradition has addressed topics such as the abolition of slavery and civil rights. It has crossed race, gender, denomination, and socio-economic barriers.

Beginning with the second part of this chapter I would like to set forth some of the facts regarding the Egypto-African contributions to Christianity and the Africanity of Jesus Christ Himself. You should readily assume that asserting the predominate presence of African pre-Christian christian thought and the Africanity of Jesus are in direct and conscious rebellion against the Euro-American slave Christian paradigm with its white Egyptians, non-African Ethiopians, Semitic or non-African (white) Hebrews, Jews, and ultimately a European Messiah. This is a Christianity which has allowed its practitioners to practice genocide around the world while paying lip service to documents promoting the philosophy and ideals of freedom. This Christianity has allowed governments of so-called Christian nations to sell and barter human beings as capital. This Christianity closes its eyes at the establishment of ghetcolonies in urban America. This Christianity promotes a hypocritical one-sided philosophy of non-violence and love while taking up arms against Third World peoples in order that the worldwide racist (white supremacy) Christian order might not topple. This Christianity has embraced a Bible translated by thirty-two racist translators under the aegis of a racist English monarch. This Christianity asks me what difference color makes when I assert the historical facts and affirm the Biblical dignity given to Africans and their descendants. This Christianity does not ask what difference color makes when drugs flown or floated into this country navigate themselves straight to African-American communities to promote violence and death. This Christianity calls Ronald Reagan a Christian while in eight years of Mr. Reagan's politics African-Americans experienced the most devastating economic set backs in post Civil War years. This Christianity seems not to be chagrined over its duplicity in promoting the Euro-American slave Christian paradigm by not questioning literature, curriculum and so-called art which portray Biblical characters in a historically inaccurate fashion. This Christianity has been taught in seminaries whose commitment to status-quoism forbid them to develop strong theological perspectives which grapple with the Anglo-centricity of the Biblical academy and causes them to fear the re-thinking, re-writing and re-articulating of history.

African Foundations
of Christianity
(Part II)

I would suggest that the particularly Western brand of "Christianity" is not all associated with the Jesus Christ of Scripture or history. It is implicitly oppressive and particularly inimical to the complete humanization of peoples of color worldwide. In their book "What Color Is Your God," Columbus Salley and Ronald Behm write: "Christianity as the national religion has become synonomous with the oppressive institutions of White racism which seek to perpetuate the social, economic and political subordination of Black Americans. It has, in effect, done its greatest damage in conditioning Black people to hate themselves and all things associated with Blackness. People who hate themselves are not psychologically equipped to function as equal and potent members of any society."

Major J. Jones in "The Color of God" wrote: "Since 1619 and too often, Black Afro-Christians have had to cope with a Western concept of God which implied that God is white. Without a clear, Black God-concept, stripped of White connotations, a Black person is not free to worship or affirm God as one with whom that Black person can completely identify. By manipulating the White God-concept, many White people have sought to control Black people's thinking, even to the point of setting them against their own blackness." Jones further states, "If one cannot free God of alien connotations, then one cannot affirm one's personal, full humanity. To be free of the ex-master the former slave must cease to embrace the master's highest symbol of identification: the slaveholder's God. Does it not always follow that the inner subjectivity of Afro-American people, of which their blackness is an inseparable part is a source of the deepest truth about themselves and their God. The extent to which their God is free of alien connotations is the measure of that people's freedom....God and human development are not viewed as separate and counter, but rather as complimentary to each other."

"Christianity" in America and other European countries inasmuch as it, as a system propagates a paradigm, *zeitgeist, weltanschauung,* a stronghold of deliberately falsified history, promotes ideologically based interpretations of Scriptures and promotes a dubious, unbiblical nonincarnational spirituality must be rejected. The Apostle Paul in II Corinthians 13:5 exhorts us to "Examine yourselves to see whether you are in the faith; test yourselves...." Many African-American and Anglo-Americans do not understand the disenchantment and cynicism, the contempt in which "Christianity" was held by such leaders as the Honorable Marcus M. Garvey, the Honorable Elijah Muhammad, and Malcolm X. When one diligently studies the historical record of what Whites have done to African-Americans, to Third World peoples and to one another in the name of God, Christ, the Bible and the Church, one is tempted to hurl obscenities at God or to free Him from the morass of lies called Western theology and Christianity.

In his extremely valuable work "The Arrogance of Faith," Forest G. Wood has written, "...Christian thought and conduct in the first three centuries of American life came down overwhelmingly on the side of human oppression." Christianity's infamous relationship with Africa goes back to the persecution of the first several centuries A.D." Lothrop Stoddard wrote, "In so far as he is Christianized, the Negro's savage instincts will be restrained and he will be disposed to acquiesce in white tutelage." (Lothrop Stoddard, "The Rising Tide of Colour)

In "The Black Presence in the Bible" Rev. Walter A. McCray quotes Dr. Charles B. Copher who states: "Granted that the Bible, along with interpretations of it, have proved to be and continue to be sources of blessings to millions of people. It is also true that those have been and continue to be some of the greatest curses humankind has known...In no instance...has the Bible and interpretations of it led to such murder-physical, psychological, social, and spiritual-as in the case of Black people...such murder goes back to ancient times and is still being committed today" (McCray: 1990).

Western Christianity with its racist interpretations of the Bible, its Euro-centric liturgies, icons, and white-washed African martyrs and scholars is the most successful and longest running propaganda machine in the history of the world.

John Hope Franklin, the eminent scholar of history has written, "Ministers were encouraged to instruct the slaves along the lines of obedience and subserviency....In the last three decades before the Civil War the church that had found refuge and solace in the religious instructions of the white clergy had reason to believe that they were now trapped by an enemy that had once befriended them" (John Hope Franklin: 1947,1988).

A statement made by Joseph L. White in his book "The Psychology of Blacks" betrays what I believe to be the dysfunctionalism of particularly African in America. "Christianity." He refers to this "Christianity" as being in content...Euro-American, but the style and form shows a definite African influence." (White:1984) The African influence is upon the "worship," and the style of preaching is Euro-American. This is dangerous dualism. African-Americans who worship African-American but think Biblically as Euro-Americans.

David Walker, whose pamphlet entitled "Appeal to the Coloured Citizens of the World" but in particular and very expressly, to those of The United States of America, was published in 1829 sparked an anti-slavery campaign that was militant and revolutionary. In Article III of Walker's Appeal he asks, "can anything be a greater mockery of religion than the way in which it is conducted by Americans?"

An entire volume could be written on the atrocities committed against African peoples and peoples of color around the world. However, I am at present more interested in the cumulative psychological effects of the dysfunctional Euro-American slave "Christianity" upon African Americans and Whites in America.

At the beginning of this book we set out to correct historical falsification of the Biblical record. To proclaim the copious literature attesting to the African origin of civilization. Now we must go on to examine the fact that the "Christian" faith which has been used to dehumanize and Christianize (i.e. narcotize) African American and White (European) "Christians" has its doctrinal and philosophical antecedents in Ethiopia and Egypt. What a great irony of history. Of course it was the original belief system of Jesus, His disciples and the early church which has its genesis in Ethiopia and Egypt, not racist, counterfeit Christianity!

Now you may ask why it is necessary to set the historical record straight. Well first of all, it is precisely because it is the historical record that it needs to be set straight. Secondly, because a faith which depends upon history, as does true Christianity, needs to appeal to the historical verifiability of its claims.

Christianity was not born of a virgin, and it bears repeating that the underpinings of Christianity are African. It may even be established that God's original people, the Hebrews were of a mixed African stock. Often the

"Jewishness" of Jesus Christ is used as a statement of the non-Whiteness or non-Blackness of Jesus. This is extremely ridiculous, makes no point, and falls utterly apart when one is able to establish the African element in the early Hebrews and then trace it right down to Mary, Joseph, and ultimately to Jesus Himself. A further example of the futility of the Jesus was a Jew argument is that within its context Jewishness becomes an ambiguous non-ethnic classification for a man who clearly had a racial and ethnic heritage which He made no attempt to hide.

In "The Black Messiah," Rev. Albert Cleage, Jr. has written: "The nation of Israel was mixture of Chaldeans, Egyptians, Midianites, Ethiopians, Kushites, Babylonians, and other dark peoples, all of whom were already mixed with the black people of Central Africa."

Every preacher in America should have in his library John L. Johnson's "The Black Biblical Heritage." On p. 235, Mr. Johnson writes, "The original Hebrews had black skin. For centuries, they lived around Black Egyptians, Ethiopians, Canaanites, and other Negro stocks. At one time Hebrews, Egyptians, Ethiopians, Canaanites, and other African tribes were very difficult to distinguish from each other, if documentary (birth record) proof was not available. Usually in such situations, the Hebrews were distinguished by their dialect, dwelling area, and religion.

Walter A. McCray has stated, "...let us beware of the flawed thinking which tells us that the Biblical covenant people were not Black or White but "Jews." To assert for the sake of a color and/or ethnological argument that the Biblical covenant community were "Jews" says no more about their precise anthropological/ethnological composition and appearance relative to their Black kindredness as though our saying that they were "Semitic." Incidentally some scholars assert that "Semitic" or "Semite" is a linguistic rather that ethnic designation.

Again this discussion is important because "Christianity" or for our purposes, belief, or Bible faith stands or falls with our understanding of who Jesus was and is.

Sir E. A. Wallis Budge, revered Egyptologist and prodigious author wrote, "There is little doubt that in her character of the loving protecting mother she appealed strongly to the imagination of all the...peoples among her cult...and that the pictures and sculptures wherein she is represented in the act of suckling Horus formed the foundation for the Christian painting of the Madonna and Child" (Budge, "The God of the Egyptians" Dover, 1969).

Professor George G. M. James explains in his classic work "Stolen Legacy" "The statue of the Egyptian Goddess Isis with her child Horus in her arms was the first Madonna and Child."

John G. Jackson in "Christianity Before Christ" quotes Dr. Alvin Boyd Kuhn who writes: "The entire Christian Bible, creation legend, descent into and exodus from Egypt, ark and flood allegory, Israelite history, Hebrew prophecy and poetry, Gospels, Epistles and Revelation imagery, all are now proven to have been the transmission of ancient Egypt's scrolls and papyri into the hands of later generations which knew neither their true origin nor their fathomless meaning." Kuhn further states: "Egypt had used the symbol of a star rising in the east as the portent of coming deity for milennia anterior to the Christian era. Egypt had knelt at the shrine of the Madonna and Child, Isis and Horus, for long centuries before a historical Mary lifted a historical Jesus in her arms. Egypt had from remote times adored a Christ who had raised the dead and healed the lame, halt, blind, paralytic, leprous and all afflicted, who had restored speech to the dumb, exorcised demons from the possessed, dispersed His enemies with a word or look, wrestled with His Satan adversary, overcame all temptation and performed the works of His heavenly Father to the victorious end."

Professor Albert Churchward in "Origin and Evolution of Religion" wrote: "The mystery of the resurrection was originally instituted by these Totemic Nilotic Negroes, may be seen still symbolically by the Arunta Tribes. Every native has to pass through certain ceremonies before he is admitted to the secrets of the tribe. The first takes place at about the age of twelve years; the final and most impressive one is not passed through until the native has reached the age of thirty years" (Churchward 1924).

The stalwart North African theologian Augustine wrote in the "Retractto" "That which is known as the Christian religion existed among the ancients, and never did not exist; from the beginning of the human race until the time when Christ came in the flesh, at which time the true religion, which already existed began to be called "Christianity." It should be noted here that the Master never referred to His followers as Christians neither did He instruct anyone else to do so. The word" Christian " is found twice in Scripture, both times in the book of Acts. In both instances the word is used by unbelievers to refer derogatorily to believers.

In the "Journal of African Civilizations" Professor John Jackson tells us that: "Gerald Massey, and his school, have argued persuasively for an Egyptian Origin of Christianity, claiming that the whole Christian Bible, both Old and New Testaments are traceable to the religious records of ancient Egypt" (*Journal of African Civilizations* Nov. 1982). In the appendix to "Ancient Egypt" the same Gerald Massey lists more than two hundred parallels between Jesus and the Osiris-Horus cycle. Let it be stated soundly and unequivocally that Horus was not the Christ. He possessed no divinity nor had he power to forgive sin. There is no salvation in the name of Horus.

Dr. Albert Churchward tells us, "Horus was with his mother, the virgin, until twelve years old, when he was transformed into the beloved son of God, as the only begotten of the Father in Heaven." Allow me to set the

73

record straight by saying that I absolutely do not believe that Horus was the only begotten of the Father. That distinction belongs to the Jesus Christ of Scripture and history who was born in Bethlehem Judah to Mary and Joseph. (Micah 5:2; Matthew 1:18-24) The fact that Horus was and is not the Savior of the world is not the point of emphasis. The point is that Christianity as a system of codified thought had strong Egyptian antecedents.

It had been written also that on the inner walls of the holy chamber of the Temple of Luxor, called curiously enough the holy of holies, there are some inscriptions. Supposedly the birth of Horus is depicted in four scenes which are very similar to the Anunciation; the Immaculate Conception; the Birth of the Child; and the Adoration. (Gerald Massey, "Ancient Egypt: The Light of the World" Vol II p. 757).

The late Will Durant in Vol IV of the "Story of Civilization" wrote: "Statues of Isis and Horus were renamed Mary and Jesus; the Roman Lupercalia and the feast of the Purification of Isis became the Feast of the Nativity; the Saturnalia were replaced by Christmas celebration."

Given contemporary "artistic" depictions of Jesus, Mary and the disciples we find it curious that in fifteen centuries of art after the founding of the Church one finds no non-black depictions of Jesus Christ or the Virgin Mary.

Matthew 1:14-15 says, "So he got up, took the child and his mother and left for Egypt, where he stayed until the death of Herod. And so was fulfilled what the Lord had said through the prophet: Out of Egypt I called my son."

In his book "Images of Jesus" Anton Wessels writes, "Jesus was in Africa before the rise of Christianity. After all, the Holy Family had to flee to Egypt and, according to tradition stayed there for six months." Joseph, Mary and Jesus went into Egypt, the historic home of the Kemetic or black faced people for a sojourn of approximately six months. Of Jesus raciality John L. Johnson has written,

"Jesus was God in an earthly body...He was not a "pure Jew" of the flesh for there were many Hamitic Blacks in His earthly genealogy....According to the Scriptures, from Abraham (father of the David line) up until King Solomon, Hebrews of that lineage took many black sons and daughters of Ham to be their mates."

Jesus in Revelation 5:5 is referred to as..."the Lion of the tribe of Judah, the Root of David...." The tribe of Judah, was not without an African (Black) presence. Judges 1:16-19 says: "The descendants of Moses' father-in-law, the Kenite, went up from the City of Palms (Jericho) with the men of Judah to live among the people of the Desert of Judah in the Negev near Arad. Then the men of Judah went with the Simeonites their brothers and attached the Canaanites living in Zephath, and they totally destroyed the city. Therefore, it was called Hormah.

The men of Judah also took Gaza, Ashkelon, and Ekron-each city with its territory. The Lord was with the men of Judah. They took possession of the hill country..." Judah, including its Kenite (African) segment, was mighty in war with the Canaanites.

There was a need for Jesus to go into Egypt. Matthew 1:21 says of Mary, "She will give birth to a son, and you are to give him the name Jesus, because he will save his people from their sins." There were people, Jesus' people in Egypt, who rejoiced over His birth. Isaiah 11:10-11 says, "In that day the Root of Jesse will stand as a banner for the peoples; the nations will rally to him, and his place of rest will be glorious. In that day the Lord will reach out his hand a second time to claim the remnant that is left of his people from Assyria, from Lower Egypt, from Upper Egypt, (Mitzraim) from Cush, (Ethiopia) from Elam, from Babylonia, from Hamath and from the islands of the sea." The Lord is naming and claiming His people from among the Black nations of the world.

At a conference in New York where I recently spoke

there was a respectable group from "the islands of the sea." There were brothers and sisters from Curacao, Trinidad and Tobego, Jamaica, the West Indies, and Port au Prince in Haiti. One beloved brother present at the New York conference, pastors the largest church in Curacao. The black peoples in Egypt needed confirmation that Christ was born, that their deliverer was indeed alive, prophecy had been fulfilled.

Let us not forget that it was in Egypt that Israel (the Hebrews) spent 430 years in captivity. The Hebrews were also at various times carried away into captivity by Babylon, and Assyria, both black nations. They were also turned over to Cush for the discipline of their disobedience.

Judges 3:7-8 says, "The Israelites did evil in the eyes of the Lord their God and served the Baals and the Asherahs. The anger of the Lord burned against Israel so that he sold them into the hands of Cushan-Rishathaim king of Aram Naharaim, to whom the Israelites were subject for eight years." These were periods of intense widespread racial mixture and even Exodus 12:38 tells us that the Hebrews came out of Egypt as "a mixed multitude." This truth is further supported by Leviticus 24:10 which says, "Now the son of an Israelite mother and an Egyptian father went out from among the Israelites..." Yes, there was much mixing among Hebrews when father, Abraham, was from black Ur of the Chaldeans, descendants of the Sumerians who referred to themselves as the Blackheads.

In Revelation 1:15 John writes, "His feet were like bronze glowing in a furnace..." (NIV). The King James states that His feet were as burnt brass. Anyone who has taken basic chemistry knows that burnt brass takes on a blackish hue.

John G. Jackson in "Was Jesus Christ a Negro?" quotes Kersey Graves who stated: "There is much evidence that the Christian Savior was a black man, or at least a dark

76

man, as there is of his being the son of the Virgin Mary." As we have noted earlier, there is not one shred of evidence in sixteen centuries of painting, sculpture, and relief that Jesus and Mary were anything but of a dark brown or near black complexion with African features. Indus Khamit-Kush quotes Kersey Graves who wrote, "In the pictures and portraits of Christ by the early Christians, He (Jesus) is uniformly represented as being black." (Indus Khamit-Kush 1983)

In Volume I of J. A. Rogers' indispensible "Sex and Race" on page two hundred seventy-five Rogers writes, "A German correspondent, resident in New York City, wrote me as regards the Black Virgin of her native land, Bavaria, saying that for years she has been trying to tell Americans that Christ and the Virgin Mary were black but that they would not believe her...in our churches the biggest reference is given to Santa Maria as Mother of God and we have statues of the Madonna as well as pictures, which are original sculptures or paintings on wood and stone, dating as far back as 800 to 1,000 years and more. The faces of these images are black and of Negroid type, particularly the Madonnas, of Constuchon in Tolers and the Mother of God statue in Alt-Oltung in Bavaria near Munich, which was brought from Palestine more that 1,000 years ago by Ritter von Heiligers Lande." Also a coin dated from the reign of Justinian II shows Christ with tightly curled hair and African features. J. A. Rogers quotes the "Cambridge Encyclopedia" as saying, "Whatever the fact, this coin places beyond doubt the belief that Jesus Christ was a Negro" (J. A. Rogers 1967).

To those who contend that the issue of Jesus' raciality or ethnicity is inflammatory and racist, I beg your indulgence. As long as it has been assumed that Jesus was white, there has been no discussion. People of color have had to live with the internal tension. However, more recent scholarship has given as reason to open a lively discussion over just who Jesus really was. This is the central issue of our faith, who was Jesus Christ of Nazareth, Son of the Living God? It really should not be an issue. However, the history of racism and the advantage false religion has gained in the African-American community due to the Eurocentricity of Christianity render historical accuracy imperative. For those, again, who cite the "Jewishness" of Jesus as non-black, non-white category of distinction I offer you the following. William Mosley wrote a fine book entitled "What Color was Jesus?" In that book Mr. Mosley writes, "Arthur Koestler, a Scottish scholar,...demonstrates in the "The Thirteenth Tribe" that there were no European Jews until the 7th century A.D. Everybody in the Old Testament was African (Black) and no white person appears until mention is made of the Roman occupation."

You see the image of white Jesus has devastating implications for all people, both believers and non-believers. Particularly since such an image has no Biblical, archeological or historical support. The perpetuation of white images of not only Jesus Christ but a host of other prominent Biblical characters has a disastrous effect on Bible scholarship, preaching, teaching, Christian living, worship and evangelism. It also affects creativity, the realm of the arts, poetry, drama, painting, music, sculpture, rhetoric. There is also a potential impact upon business and a proper understanding of true spirituality. I will look more in depth at some of these issues in the next chapter.

SEVEN

The Black Hebrews

Most Americans believe that the historical relationship between Africa and the Church began with the so-called missionaries of the west. This is one more example of a deliberately falsified history.Ethiopia is the oldest Christian nation in the world and Christianity was spread across Africa when there was no west(as presently defined). In this chapter we will look back at the origins of Christianity in Africa. When one understands that the original Hebrews were an African people then the presence of Christianity in Africa early on is not so surprising.

Bishop A. G. Dunston, Jr. has written, "What are we to conclude when people as late as 20 A.D. looked at Jesus and believed themselves to have been descendants of the Ethiopians? The Greek term "Ethiopia means "black" or literally "burnt faced," and the only way to decide that a person or a people were Ethiopians would be by sight identification. The fact that the opinion was not ridiculous to Tacitus must have been because it supported what he saw when he saw Israelites."

Jose' V. Malcioln in his book "How the Hebrews Became Jews," stated the following concerning the Hebrew people, "Studies show that the people were Hamitic and migrated to the east, south, southwest, and the west." There is another interesting quote from Brother Malcioln who quotes Charles Rollin: "Historians are unanimously agreed that Menes was the first king of Egypt...He is the same with Misraim, the son of Cham...Cham was the second son of Noah...After the Tower of Babel they dispersed themselves into different countries, Cham retired to Africa...He had four children. They were Chus, Misraim, (when the Arabians call up to two day Mesre), Phut and Canaan. (The son named) Chus settled in Ethiopia, Mesraim in Egypt. Phut took possession of that part of Africa westward of Egypt (that is now Libya) and Canaan took part of that country that afterward took his name. This last one was Syria in the 13th and 14th century), it is now the coast of Palestine...." Malcioln finally states, "Mystical and mythological ties can be eliminated when we recall that the Iberian Peninsula was named after the Iberian (not a Caucasian, as some historians state, but "a short black man, with curly hair, frugal, obstinate, and revengeful, who came across to Spain from North Africa)" (Jose' V. Malcioln, 1978). There are many people in Mexico who pray both in Hebrew and Spanish. Also bear in mind that Africans were in Mexico 700 years before Europeans and that most of the major Mexican gods including Teccatlipoca, are black. The presence of people in Mexico who pray in both Hebrew and the tongue of their Mexican brothers and sisters testifies to the far-reachedness of the African Diaspora. The question should be asked whether there is any link between the African and Jewish Diasporas.

In "From Babylon to Timbuktu" Rudolph R. Windsor writes, "Originally all Hamites and Shemites (or Semites) wore black. Abraham was a black Shemite and a descendant of Shem...Abraham was the father not only of the Hebrew-Israelite nation, but also of the Arab nation." Windsor further states: "The black Jews of India, Abyssinia (Ethiopia), and West Africa consider themselves the original Jews because of the purity of their Israelite blood; this has been stated by Allen H Godbey."

It is important to understand the Africanity of the original Hebrews for other than purely historic reasons. If, as we have been taught, Judaism was somewhat the womb of Christianity, then a black (African) mother will give birth to a black (African) baby. Specific and copious Hebrewisms are found throughout Africa even to this very day. So it is important if we accept ancient Hebrew worship as progressively leading to Christ to understand the foundations of Christ worship. In the last chapter we noted some parallels between Biblical monotheists, Abraham and Moses, were black. We should also remember that the Hebrew Israelite nation was born in Egypt.

Here I need to point out something very significant. Genesis 38:1-2 says, "At that time, Judah left his brothers and went to stay with a man of Adullam named Hirah. There Judah met the daughter of a Canaanite man named Shua. He married her and lay with her; she became pregnant and gave birth to a son and named him Onan. She gave birth to still another son and named him Shelah. It was at Kenih that she gave birth to him."

Er, means watchful. Onan, means strong. Shelah, or Salah means missile or javelin. Now the Bible says that Judah's father-in-law was Shua. In order to identify Shua let us look at Genesis 25:1-2, "Abraham took another wife whose name was Keturah. She bore him...Shuah." Shua, Judah's father-in-law was Abraham's son.

The first wife of Judah (Praise) was a black Canaanite woman whose father was a descendant of Abraham. Please note that this Canaanite woman who married Judah was fertile to bring forth sons. Sons imply patriarchy. Patriarchy, when covenant is kept, implies stability, rulership, generational wealth and wisdom and the overall blessings of God. Psalm 127:3-5 says: "Sons are a heritage from the Lord, children a reward from him. Like arrows

81

in the hands of a warrior are sons born in one's youth. Blessed is the man whose quiver is full of them. They will not be put to shame when they contend with their enemies in the gate." Verse four is significant, "Like arrows in the hands of a warrior are sons born in one's youth," when you remember that Shelah means javelin or missile.

I pray that my precious African sisters are not offended by all the gender specific language. Please note that it is of God that your men should be restored to strength, dignity and honour so that you may return unto your throne. God has a word for you in the story of Esther and Mordecai. However, let me speak to my African sisters in love. You must return to the House of God, you must lie with Judah. "Lie" or "lay" in Hebrew means to lie down for rest or sexual connection; to overlay one's self, to lodge, take rest or stay. Many of our sisters are too busy, they are not lying, resting, lodging, and overlaying themselves with Judah (Praise).

You are daughters of Abraham, overlay yourselves with praise and become pregnant. When the African segment of the body begins to lie with praise she will bring forth sons. With the dismal statistics facing black males, the Church needs to begin to lie with Judah to bring forth spiritual sons who are strong, watchful and as missiles in their father's quiver to the next generations.

I need to wrap this up and get back to our initial thrust, however, this truth about praise is important. The statement I am about to make must be taken in context and in the spirit of love and understanding. Genesis 38 tells us that after Judah was separated from the Canaanite woman by her death he got in trouble. He was lured into a sexual liason with a prostitute who was his daughter-in-law disguised. You see, Judah did not release his seed to be joined to his wife. He violated spiritual protocol, misunderstood his measure of rule. As a result of Judah's actions Tamar's womb brought forth division and strife.

Now in our day Judah must be restored because it is the tribe from which the roaring Lion has come. A fresh wind of the Spirit is blowing about Judah. In order for the African segment of the body of Christ to wave and usher in God's purpose we must sanctify ourselves and hear from God afresh. I believe that the Father would have us no longer sing songs of slavery, and torment, but that He would put into our hearts and mouths the word of prophetic songs, songs of victory and encouragement. That God would raise up in the African American segment of the Body of Christ sons of Asaph and Heman, prophetic musicians ordained and positioned in the House of God by the King. Only this time Judah will not seek out the prostitues of rock and roll, ryhthm and blues, and the panting, lustful perversions of God's holy gifts. There is much more we could say on this, but the most important thing is that we know the Black man as Hebrew-Israelite flows throughout the Bible with an undeniable presence. This presence carries over into the early Christian Church.

More data supporting the Africanity, the blackness of the early Hebrew-Israelite nation comes from Sterling M. Means. He writes: "The Jews were the first nation to branch off from the Black and the most striking proofs of this fact is that there are Black Jews still found in Africa and India. They have their Asiatic features and speak the Hebrew language, and I have often heard they are more accurate in their tradition than Jews elsewhere. The African and Indian Jews belong to the branch, Ur of the Chaldees with Abraham." Means writes further, "The Chaldeans were a Kushite nation and the word Kush is a Hebrew word for Ethiopia which shows that the Jews descended from the Ethiopian race" (Sterling M. Means, "Ethiopia and the Missing Link in African History" 1945). In fairness Ethiopia is probably a Greek word not a Hebrew word, however, the meaning does not change.

My brother and sister you need to know that the

ancient Hebrew-Israelite nation was a Black nation born in Egypt. Remember that Israel was the name of a person before it came to designate a specific geographic locale. The nation itself is of the loins of black Abraham from Ur of the (black) Chaldean people. No matter how you shake it you cannot get a caucasian or so-called Semitic people. The people who emerged from Egypt by force of circumstance had to have been a people of various shades of black, brown, and brown-red.

The reader should be advised that the author has chosen to quote the sources so copiously so as to render quaint dismissal of the facts impossible. I am attempting to spread before you a sumptuous banquet of historical and anthropological research that you may feast upon until your appetite is satisfied.

Abraham was foretold by God of the dispersion of the Hebrew people around the world. This dispersion has been called the Jewish Diaspora. In his very important book "Hebrewism of West Africa," Joseph J. Williams has written: "After a general consideration of the Diaspora itself, the first line of investigation led from the Abyssinian centre of Hebraic influence, that dates back to a more or less legendary origin, and which eventually built up the distinctively Jewish Falashas." The Abyssinians were a Black people and the Falashas are the recently much discussed Ethiopian Jews. It is interesting to note that these Ethiopian Jews (Falashas) refer to themselves as Beta-Israel. In the eighteenth century the Beta-Israel has and used the same copy of the Old Testament Scriptures as the Abyssinians Christians; it was called the Geez. It is also noteworthy that Beta-Israel produced a body of important literature. Among that literature is the Te'ezaza Sanbat or The Commandants of the Sabbath. In this work is included the stories of Creation, the Garden of Eden, Abraham, Noah, Moses, and others.

It has been established that long before Titus' destruction of the Temple in 70 A.D. the Mediterranean shore of Africa was populated with influental Jewish colonies. Egypt had become a place of refuge for those fleeing Jerusalem at the time of the Babylonian Captivity. A strong Hebrew influence is known to have penetrated West Africa where many Hebrewisms may still be observed among non-Islamized peoples.

Joseph J. Williams quotes John B. Deane who concluded "...there is room for one of these two conclusions; that the Gold Coast was either colonized from Canaan, or from Egypt, the former of which is perhaps more probable, from the greater facility afforded to the Phoenicians by navigation than to the Egyptians...." The early Hebrew-Israelite nation which was born in Egypt and through the Diaspora populated Canaan and Africa to its interior was a Black nation.

Now when we see the Jewish or the Hebrew Diaspora as a worldwide dispersal or distribution not of Caucasians but of Africans and Afro-Asiatics, our thinking must change radically concerning the regathering of the Jews and the relevance of the Hebrew faith to Christianity. Passages such as Isaiah 11:10-11 speak of the regathering of the people of God. Isaiah says:"...In that day the Lord will reach out his hand a second time to reclaim the remnant that is left of his people from Assyria, from Lower Egypt, from Upper Egypt, from Cush, from Elam, from Babylonia, from Hamath and from the islands of the sea." God's great black people are dispersed around the world awaiting the regathering.

On page 131 of Joseph Williams "Hebrewism of West Africa" the author makes the following statements; "...the wanderings of that race or people whose dispersion is regarded by some as the means chosen by Divine Providence to prepare the way for Christianity, by drawing back to the primitive monotheistic idea the pagan world that had become corrupt, and through unbridled lusts sunk deep into polytheistic practices of sensuous idolatry." The Hebrew-Israelite nation was chosen by God to show God to the world. They were to demonstrate by keeping of God's covenants His forgiveness, justice, judgement, mercy, prosperity and equity. These people were God's peculiar and treasured possessions (Exodus 19:5-6).

Over decades and centuries these Hebrews encountered groups of people who were lighter complexioned due to migrating realities. This, the Hebrew-Israelite nation which had once been Black by what we know to be racial or phenotypical distinctions was no longer such. However, its Ethio-Egyptian roots never did change.

As it relates to Egypt where the Hebrew-Israelite nation was born, weakening internal political strength invited the first Asian incursions into Ethiopia and Egypt. These Asians incursions were most extreme between 2181-2040 B.C. during the eighth, ninth, and tenth dynasties. This disunity between Upper and Lower Egypt encouraged Asians who had already invaded and replaced the Libyan population to march across the desert. Ultimately these Asians were able also to displace the indigenous population. During this period non-integrating Blacks moved southward below the First Cataract. This Asian expansion occured during an age of weak kings in the aforementioned dynasties.

Finally in 2040 B.C. Mentuhotep II the greatest of the Eleventh Dynasty kings, reversed integration policies and expelled the invaders. This established another "Golden Age" of African rule. Another invasion occured in 1720 B.C. when more Asian and probably Mediterranean (proto-Caucasian) marauders came into Egypt wreaking havoc and destruction. Intense intermarrying and interbreeding took place during these periods thus the differing appearances of the Ethiopians, Egyptians and Hebrews.

I was asked recently, "How, if the ancient Hebrew

Israelites were Black, have we come to the blond haired, blue-eyed Jews of today?" I believe a quote from the venerable Bishop Alfred G. Dunston will answer the question. He writes, "Today we see white descendants of the Children of Israel because many of them settled in Europe as the Muslims invaded the Middle East and many others fled deeper into Europe as the Muslims conquered Spain and marched half way across France. There can be no objection to the idea that European intermarriage contributed a great deal to the appearance of the Jews during the early Christian era and during the Middle Ages."

The importance of this chapter on the Black Hebrews makes repetition necessary. Notice repetition not redundance. African-American Christians must stop reading the Bible while experiencing a cognitive and experiential disassociation from its history. Our ancestors adorn the pages of the Bible and its history from Genesis to Revelation, from the Davidic Kingdom to the disciples of Jesus, from the prophets to the prophets.

I should note something interesting here. At the time of the Exodus, 430 years after the original seventy had gone into Egypt, the Hebrew-Israelite nation had grown to over 600,000. (Exodus 12:37) It would seem next to impossible humanly speaking, that seventy could multiply to six hundred thousand in four hundred thirty years. Some scholars suggest that the actual sojourn was only two hundred fifty years making the feat of multiplication even more incredible. The intensive breeding could only take place by having more than the original seventy reproducing. Exodus 12:38 says, "And a mixed multitude went up also with them." This group was most assuredly mixed in race, color, and national origin.

Marriage prohibitions placed upon the Hebrew-Israelite nation by God had nothing to do with race and everything to do with worship and religious practices. In Deuteronomy 7:1-2 God commands His people, the Hebrew-Israelite nation, to totally exterminate the seven Canaanite nations of the Promised Land and obviously to contract no marriage with them. However, with other nations outside the Promised Land treaties might be made (Deuteronomy 20:11). Also Deuteronomy 23:7-8 says, "Do not abhor an Edomite, for he is your brother. Do not abhor an Egyptian because you lived as an alien in his country. The third generation of children born to them may enter the assembly of the Lord." Joseph J. Williams quotes George Fost Moore: "The Canaanite population had been absorbed in Israel by intermarriage." He also quotes John Pederson who wrote, "A non-Israelite city, Jerusalem, was made the capitol of the country, and David surrounded himself with many foreigners. He was the ruler of a country and an empire, and we hear of no antagonism between Israelites and Canaanites as they merged into the Israelite unity and disappeared, naturally infusing Canaanite life and culture into Israel."

The Biblically established, historically verified racial, national and phenotypical diversity among the original Hebrew-Israelite nation establishes a very relevant point. This nation was never intended to be racially homogenous; it was a covenant nation.

There is no hidden agenda of racial supremacy in my work. I do not believe in the inherent superiority or inferiority of any one group of humans. We are one race, the human race, with beautiful and unique ethnic subdivisions. I have a single motive and that is to correct hundreds of years of distorted history. This falsified history has been the foundation of racism with all its ugly and not yet annihilated consequences. It is truth that will free the spirits, souls, and bodies of God's people. The burden of my heart is to see all the saints perfected. We in the African-American segment of the Body must make our calling and election sure. God has always been active in history and in this hour He is restoring truth that will restore African peoples. Welfare, decaying cities, teenage pregnancy, and loss of hope are not our legacy. It is needful that we write and excavate the powerful Black African, and African-American presence in both Biblical and world history. Black people are a spiritual people. We need suffer the pain of demonic distortions of history no longer. God has breathed upon us, the hour of our liberation is upon us. We are not "minorities" or negroes, negras, or colored. We are of Royal Ethio-Egyptian Hebrew descent, literally a major part of the People of God.

An even stronger argument that has been presented here could be made in support of the strong and dense Black presence among the Hebrew-Israelite nation even hundreds of years after their exclusively Black Egyptian origins (see Habakkuk 3:7; Judges 3:8; I Samuel 30:29; Judges 4:17; I Chronicles 2:55; Jeremiah 35).

Finally, in an essay entitled "Three Thousand Years of Biblical Interpretation with Reference to Black Peoples" the distinguished scholar Charles B. Copher concluded, "...the Old Testament especially is a collection of writings by and about Black people."

EIGHT

Africa and Early Christianity

The New Testament Church was born in Jerusalem. Acts 2:5-11 (NIV) says, "Now there were staying in Jerusalem God-fearing Jews from every nation under heaven. When they heard this sound, a crowd came together in bewilderment, because each one heard them speaking in his own language. Utterly amazed, they asked: "Are not these men who are speaking Galileans? Then how is it that each of us hears them in his own native language? Partuam, Medes, Elamites, residents of Mesopotamia, Judea, and Capodecia, Pontus and Asia, Phrygia and Pamphylia, Egypt and the parts of Libya near Cyrene; visitors from Rome (both Jews and converts to Judaism); Cretans and Arabs-we hear them declaring the wonders of God in our own tongues."

We need to make an important geographical note about Jerusalem. According to Peters' Projection, a map formulated by German cartographer Arno Peters, Jerusalem lay at the extreme north northeast tip of Egypt not far from Cairo and Alexandria. There is a note on Peters Projection which reads as follows: "Five thousand years of human history have brought us to the threshold of a new age. It is an age typified by science and technology, by the end of colonial domination; by a growing awareness of the interdependence of all nations and all peoples. Such a moment in history demands that we look critically at our understanding of the world. This understanding is based, to a significant degree, on the work of map-makers of the age when Europe dominated and exploited the world. The work of German historian Arno Peters provides a helpful corrective to the distortions of traditional maps. While the Peters Map is superior in its portrayal of proportions and sizes, its importance goes far beyond questions of cartographic accuracy. Nothing less than our world view is at stake!" So you see that not only has history been falsified but so has geography and cartography (map-making).

Jerusalem had a history before Israel. It was a city of the Jebusites, a black Canaanite tribe. It was conquered under David and made the capital city of the Davidic Kingdom. Jerusalem was then also "the fortress of Zion," of "the City of David" (II Samuel 5:7). II Samuel 5:9-10 says, "David then took residence in the fortress and called it the City of David. He built up the area around it, from the supporting terraces inward. And he became more and more powerful, because the Lord Almighty was with him."

It is commonly assumed by contemporary Western Christians that David captured and took over a city called Jerusalem or City of Peace. This cannot be substantiated historically or linguistically. The Egyptian Execration Texts c. 1850 B.C.E. (Before the Christian Era) indicated that the city was called Urushalim or Shalem. Shalem was the local god of pre-Israelite Canaan. This god was identified with other Canaanite gods Molech and Ashtar. These gods were manifestations of the Canaanites international god, Baal. Shalem also symbolized Venus, the evening star. Shalem in the Canaanite language meant "completion." In time shalem came to be identified with a place

Jerusalem and with the nation of completion. The Israelite word shalom has its base in shalem. However, it is erroneous to refer to as Jeru-shalem what would be referred to as Jeru-shalom.

When David captured the city he added the name of the one God Yahweh in the shortened form of Ya to the city's name of Shalem. Thus David does not substitute Yahweh's name for Shalem's, he simply pre-fixes Shalem with Ya. Thus, this city is to be both the literal and symbolic place of conflict and confrontation between the forces of Yahweh and the forces of Baal.

Jerusalem, where the New Testament Church was born, had a long history of interracting with the Black Biblical presence. Of the sixteen nations mentioned in Acts 2:9-11, eleven were of conspicuous Black descent and the others had no claim to any nation of non-Black or non-Brown racial purity.

It is interesting that though we have been taught that the Ethiopian eunuch was a Gentile the Bible does not say that he was. Acts 8:26-27 says, "Now an angel of the Lord said to Philip, "Go south to the road-the desert road-that goes down from Jerusalem to Gaya. So he started out, and on his way he met an Ethiopian eunuch, an important official in charge of all the treasury of Candace, queen of the Ethiopians. This man had gone to Jerusalem to worship."

Let us not overlook the fact that Philip accosted the Ethiopian eunuch on his way to Jerusalem to worship. Worship whom? The Living God of course. With him the eunuch had a copy of the Old Testament scrolls. We know that there were no printing presses at the time and that written manuscripts were produced through painstaking labor and were extremely valuable. Also because of the eunuch's position we know that he could read and write. Now we must also assume that the eunuch was at least bilingual, speaking the tongue indigenous to his homeland of Ethiopia and also the Hebrew tongue. Or was the Hebrew tongue the tongue of the Ethiopian's land? In fact, there is a tradition which says that the Ethiopian eunuch converted by Philip was a Jew named Djan Darada, said to have been the chief steward of Queen Garsemat IV of the ancient Kingdom of Axum. Axum antedates the beginning of the Church in Jerusalem and by the forth century A.D. had become the dominant Kingdom in northeastern Africa. Another tradition identifies the eunuch as a Jewish nobleman named Juda, a chief steward in Axum under Queen Judith. Both traditions however, identify the Ethiopian eunuch as having been Jewish. If these legends carry any weight and many scholars believe they do, then the Ethiopian eunuch was not the first Gentile convert but rather a converted Black African Jew. Djan or Juda is believed to have been the first one to preach Christ in Ethiopia.

Chancellor Williams has written: "Africa was naturally among the first areas to which Christianity spread. It was next door to Palestine, and from the earliest times there had been the closest relations between the Jews and the Blacks, both friendly and hostile. The exchange of pre-Christian religious concepts took place easily and, due to the residence of so many ancient Jewish leaders in Ethiopia-Abraham, Joseph and his brothers, Mary and Jesus. The great lawgiver, Moses, was not only born in Africa but he was also married to the daughter of an African priest. The pathway for the early Christian church in the Land of the Blacks had been made smooth many centuries before." (Williams 1987)

John G. Jackson has stated: "Africans played a major role in the formalative development of both Christianity and Islam. Many aspects of the present-day Christian church were developed in Africa during the formative years of Christianity." (Jackson 1970)

It is noteworthy that two of the first martyrs of the

Christian church, Felicitas and Perpetua(A.D.180) were black. History also records the fact the Roman emperor with the dubious distinction of beginning the first persecution against the Church was an African named Septimius Severus. This is not very reliable however, because Septimius is said to have begun his wave of persecution in 193 A.D., which would have been thirteen years after Felicitas and Perpetua were said to have been killed. Also John Gillies, the Scottish cleric has written that the first persecution of the Romans against was started by Nero, followed by Domitian and Trajan, Hadrian, Antoninus Philosophus, and Verus, etc. (Gillies 1754, 1981 reprint). There are several possibilities as to why Gillies does not mention Septimius, the most likely being racism. However, in all fairness to Mr.Gillies, he probably had no idea that Septimius Severus Emperor of Rome was an African.

I do not know if in my life time we will be able to reverse the immeasurable spiritual, psychological, and social damage, done by the racist/white supremacy rewriting of history. However, we can not stand idly by any longer. In the Church there must be black, white, brown and red calls for truth. My white brothers must deeply examine themselves and weigh their committment to the faith against their committment to the Ethnophobic status quo.

The white washing of history has left us with a skewed picture of Rome. Rome was the world's greatest power of the time of Christ and the early church. It behooves us to remove the veil from our eyes regarding Rome so as to get a clearer picture of the early church.

Much of the territory under Roman rule was populated by Africans (Blacks); from North Africa to Spain where the Moors (Blacks) were settled. It is worthwhile to note that the first settlers to the North African coast were Canaanite traders from Tyre and Sidon. Their language was Phoenician, later called Punic by the Mediterranean, had strong Hebrew roots. It was part of this territory

94

where these black Phoenicians settled which was later colonized by the Romans and called Tripolitania (land of three cities). The three cities were Lepcis, Oea, and Sabratha. Oea you would perhaps recognize as Tripoli. Tripoli is in upper northwest Libya near Tunisia. This area the Romans dubbed Tripolitania covered over 110,000 square miles with its commercial, military importance. It was at Lepas Magna in Tripolitania that the African Emperor of Rome Septimius Severus was born on April 11, 145. These Libyans at Tripolitania were also the ancestors of the Barbers. This term barber is undesirable. It is not an indigenous African word. The word means in greco-Roman language "barbarians." These North African Carthagenians were anything but barbarians. One half hour spent examining Peters Projection would show the reader how thoroughly African most of occupied Rome was. I shall also point out that to annex the Arabian peninsula from the continent of Africa is historically, geographically dishonest. Paul Bohanan and Philip Curtin in "Africa and Africans" write, "Geologically, the whole of the Arabian peninsula must be considered as unitary with the African continent."

W. E. B. DuBois asserts, "Black Africa widely influenced Rome. Many of her great men were called "African" because of their birth, and some of those had Negro blood." (DuBois, "The World and Africa") Dr. DuBois quotes Theodor Mommsen who wrote; "It was through Africa that Christianity became the religion of the world."

The early Fathers of the Church were African. Tertulian and Cyprian were from Carthage; Arnolius was from Sicca Veneria; also Lactantuis, Minucius Felix and Augustine were African. Origen, Athanasuis and Cyrol were from the Nile valley. Many do not know that the Roman Catholic Church had at least three African (Black) popes. Victor I (187-198); Miltiades (311-314); and Gelasius I (492-496). By the fourth century the Coptic Church of the

Nile Valley had at least a hundred bishops. It was one of these bishops, Athananuis, Bishop of Alexandria, who consecrated Frumentius as Bishop of Ethiopia around 330 A.D.

Further proof of the influence of Africa upon Rome is illustrated by the fact, "Some of the most vivid examples of Ethiopian participation in Isiac cult not from Africa, but from Italy...Another view of an Isiac ritual appears in a scene on a marble relief of the early second century, at one time part of a sarcophagus on the Via Appia near Ariccia" (Frank M. Snowden 1983). This is significant because as we pointed out earlier there are significant parallels between Jesus and Horus. Horus is said to have been born of Osiris and Isis after whom the Isiac cult takes its name. So the Egyptian antecedents of Christianity had made their way via Ethiopia into Italy.

By the end of the fourth century several important diocese of the early church had been established along the Mediterranean coast of Africa. By the end of the fifth century, Christians lived along the Mediterranean coast of Africa in the nations that now populate that coast of Morocco, Tunisia, Algeria, Libya, and the United Arab Republic (Egypt). Christianity also moved up the Nile to Ethiopia and part of the Sudan (Nubia). History tells us that the Coptic church of Egypt was established by John Mark in Alexandria. There is also a tradition which says that Thomas (" Doubting Thomas ") traveled to Egypt and did some work before going on to India where there was a significant African population.

Writing in the fourth century Rufinius says that two brothers from Tyre accompanied a friend on a trip to India. The two brothers Frumentius and Aedesius, were Christians. The route they took was the familiar one through Egypt and up the Nile. They stopped at Adulis within the Axumite kingdom for rest and food and were set upon by the locals.

Frumentius and Aedesius were the only members of their party whose lives were spared. They were appointed to the king's court as secretary-treasurer and cup-bearer respectively. When the King died succession passed to his son Ezana who was then too young to rule. Frumentius and Aedesius bore governmental responsibility and tutored young Ezana in the intricacies of government and politics. They also taught him the Christian faith and upon his coronation he became a Christian. Christianity had exercised an important influence upon Axum before Frumentius and Aedesius but Ezana's father King Ella Amida (294-325 A.D.) had not been a Christian.

Axum was a highly developed state. There the Africans practiced sophisticated agriculture, enjoyed trade networks with other African and Middle Easterners, produced highly skilled architects, stone artifers, and maintained a strong army equipped with iron weapons. Ezana is said to have made Christianity the religion of his Kingdom.

After Ezana was installed as king Frumentius and Aedesius left for Syria. They passed through Alexandria where they share their success in Axum with Bishop Athanasius. Athanasius ordained Frumentius Bishop to the Axumite (Ethiopian) Kingdom.

The Bible is believed to have been translated into the Ethiopian language about 500 A.D. There are eighty-one books; 46 in the Old Testament, and 35 in the New Testament. The pictures of Mary, Jesus, John the Baptist, even the angels, are black with wooly hair.

The African (Black) presence in early Christianity is even stronger. The Egyptian (African) Church appears at the bishopric of Demetrius of Alexandria (A.D. 189-232). It was this Demetrius who appointed the African Bishops-Pantaenus, Clement, and Origen. Pantaenus founded the world-famous Catechetical School of Alexandria which as a centre of Christian scholarship was without rival in the known world. Origen, born in A.D. 185 was a student of Clement. He lectured at Rome, Caesearea, and Jerusalem and was in great demand as a Christian intellectual and writer. He is said to have written over six thousand (6,000) books. The Egyptian Anthony became the first hermit. Pachcomias also an Egyptian became the first monk establishing the first Christian monastery on an island of the Nile.

The great Tertullian was also an African. Learned in Latin, Greek and rhetoric he was keenly interested in the religious, social, cultural, and economic development of his native Carthage. When Tertullian died in A.D. 222, the African Church had almost ninety bishops. Tertullian was a spirit filled scholar/prophet.

Between 220 and 256 three important councils met at Carthage. The North African Church had become a power only second to Rome as power had shifted from Alexandria to Carthage. When the grandeur of the early Church is lectured upon, preached, or discussed the magnificent African, personages responsible for the spiritual, doctrinal, architectural, and evangelistic glory of that Church are excluded. If African-American Christians are going to be transformed from Sunday morning building goers to believers in Christ, citizens of His Kingdom, and possessors of the salvation that is in His name, we must know the truth. If we are going to prophesy under the banner of Judah to our musicians who have left the House of God, forsaken their covenant and gone a whoring after rock and roll and soul, we must know the truth.

Under Bishop Frumentius a church was built in the Axumite kingdom which is among the world's most ancient places of worship. Saint Mary of Si church was built around 340-341. It is believed to have been built on a site where a temple formerly had been where the Queen of Sheba worshipped the sun. It is my belief based on my studies that the Queen of Sheba converted to Judaism after her visit to Jerusalem.

When Francesco Alvarez, King of Portugal, visited the Axumite Kingdom between 1521-1526 the ancient Ethiopian (Axumite) church was still standing. In his journal the Portugese King described the church as "a very large and very noble church."

The late patriarch of African scholarhsip William Leo Hansberry wrote, "The success of the Ethiopian church resulted from three factors: the diligent work of early missionaries, a flexibility in the early policy of church leaders, and the support of Ethiopian kings." (Hansberry 1974)

Under severe persecution from Roman imperial policy many Egyptian, Syrian and other Christians fled for refuge to Ethiopia. Beginning during the reign of Constantine and lasting for at least three hundred years there was intense strife among Christians within the empire. During this same period Ethiopia was experiencing tremendous peace and prosperity at home and her influence and prestige abroad were flourishing. What is conspicuously absent from most Eurocentric books on Christian or Church history is the stature that Ethiopia attained relative to the entire Byzantine empire. This Byzantine empire lasted from A.D. 395-1453. It was located in southeast Europe and southwest Asia and was a division of the Roman empire. On Ethiopia during this period Professor Hansberry has written, "For in less than two hundred years after the establishment of Christianity as the state religion, Ethiopia, by the beginning of the sixth century, had attained a level of internal development and acquired a degree of external influence which placed it on a par with the Byzantine Empire as one of the greatest Christian powers of that age." I need to again quote from Professor Hansberry regarding Ethiopia's place in world affairs. He states, "As a Christian state, Ethiopia's role in international affairs was partly influenced by elements of the Queen of

Sheba legend: first, King Solomon allegedly had a prophetic dream in which God's favor passed from Israel to Ethiopia; and second, the Ark of the Covenant was abducted and placed in Axum. Both of these allegations led Ethiopians to regard their country as the second Zion, with the Monarch regarded as successor to Justin I of Byzantium (with whom Caleb of Ethiopia was an ally in the sixth century) as defender of the Christian faith." (Hansberry 1974)

The notion that the Ark of the Covenant is to this day in Ethiopia is shared by many others not all being "lay" persons. Dr. Ephraim Isaacs is an Ethiopian Hebrew who speaks, reads and writes eight languages the most obvious of which is Hebrew. Dr. Isaacs is quoted as having said in 1973 that, "The world is raving about the Dead Sea Scrolls while the Ark of the Covenant and myriads of old original Hebrew manuscripts are rotting in Ethiopia" (Jose' V. Marcioln 1978). Graham Hancock, former East African correspondent for The Economist, has written a forthcoming book entitled The Sign And The Seal. The work is subtitled The Quest For The Lost Ark Of The Covenant. It is also Mr.Hancock's conclusion that the Ark of the Covenant presently rests in Ethiopia.

There are other fascinating tidbits from Ethiopia. The Kebra Nagast or Glory of the Kings is the most important of the Ethiopian sources and contains the story of the Queen of Sheba and Solomon. The only literary work on par with the Kebra in Ethiopia is the Bible itself. James Bruce, author of "Travels to Discover the Source of the Nile" visited Ethiopia between 1769 and 1772. During these visits Bruce acquired two copies of the Kebra Nagast which he gave to the Bodleian Library at Oxford.

Bruce writes of the Queen of Sheba, "To Saba, or Azab, then, she returned with her son Menelik, whom, after keeping him some years, she sent back to his father to be instructed. Solomon did not neglect his charge; and he was anointed and crowned King of Ethiopia in the temple of Jerusalem, and at his inauguration took the name of David. After this he returned to Azab, and brought with him a colony of Jews; among whom were many doctors of the law of Moses, particularly one of each tribe, to make judges of his kingdom, from whom the present Umbares (or supreme judges, three of whom always attend the king) are said and believed to be descended. With these came also Azarias, the son of Zadok, the priest...." Bruce adds: "The Queen of Sheba died after a long reign of forty years, in 986 before Christ, placing her son Menelik upon the throne, whose posterity, the annals of Abyssinia would teach us to believe, have ever since reigned" (Joseph J. Williams, "Hebrewism of West Africa").

In case the reader is in question regarding Abyssinia we make note of its latitudinal and longitudinal coordinates. On the Peters Projection map Abyssinia is at 10 degrees north 40 degrees east which places it almost at the center of Ethiopia between Dire Davia and Addis Ababa. The Abyssinians claim that the Queen of Sheba or Saba was a Jewess and her nation Jews, before she ever travelled to Jerusalem.

Another scholar, an Egyptologist of world renown, Ernest A. Wallis-Budge has commented upon the Kebra Nagast as follows: "This work has been held in peculiar honor in Abyssinia for several centuries and throughout the country it has been, and still is, venerated by the people as containing the final proof of their descent from the Hebrew Patriarchs, and of the Kinship of their kings of the Solomonic line, with Christ, the Son of God" (Joseph J. Williams, "Hebrewisms of West Africa").

Finally James Bruce adds that the kings of Abyssinia were "Kings of the race of Solomon, descended from the Queen of Sheba, whose devise is a lion passage, proper, upon a field of gules and their motto, 'Mo Anbasa am Nizilet Solomon am negade Juda' which signifies, 'the lion of the race of Solomon and of Judah hath overcome" (James Bruce, "Travels to Discover the Source of the Nile, Bk. II). We should definitely note here that among the Babylonians Jews the highest official was the exilarch, the Head of Captivity, whose seal was originally adorned with the design of the lion of Judah.

As you can see, the historical relationship between Christianity, the early Church, and Africa is rich and romantic. However, it is a saga which by virtue of its breadth demands volumes all its own. You should know however, that the history of Africa and Christianity continues to this day.

It is during the seventh century with the invasion of the Moslems that the glory of the North African Church began to fade. By 642 Arabs had gained control of Cyrenaica. During 647-648 the Moslems invaded Tripoli (Oea in Tripolitania). Later these Arabs pushed into Tunisia and Algeria and in 672 founded the city of Kairowan as a bastion of defense against native resistance.

During this period several African chiefs converted to the Islamic faith. Among them was Tarik, governor of Mauritania who led 400 soldiers into Spain in 711. By the eighth century Moslem Arabs had risen to great power in North Africa and Spain and we witness the beginning of the disappearance of the Church in North Africa. The African Church next emerges in West Africa where it was transported between 1450 and 1750. This is another history altogether and perhaps we shall take it up at another time.

NINE

A Challenge to American Pastors

In the previous chapters we have shared quite a bit of historical data relative to the origin, accomplishments, and contributions to civilization of Black African peoples. However, data or information alone is not necessarily meaningful, it is only a beginning. Richard King, M.D. has written, "Presently black people are awakening from the spell of mental slavery, ignorance of self, and an inability to spiritually focus the mind. Black people have learned that a major key to shattering the chains of mental slavery is to know one's own history." Dr. King further states, "When one knows the true fullness of the ancestor's achievements then that person will believe that they can do the same today. When one knows what the ancestors did to develop themsleves, in order to make such great advances, then they will know how to do the same to-day....In knowing one's history one can expand the mind through the illusion of time and space, unite with ancient black priest-scientist ancestors and utilize the same time-less and universal ideas to produce the same greatness." (Richard King, M.D., "African Origin of Biological Psy-chiatry" 1990)

I have said earlier that so-called Christianity deliber-ately founded upon a lie is dysfunctional and serves the status quo. The deliverance of Black or African-American Christians is not going to come from having hands laid upon them by some sawdust trail evangelist, or even by some designer Hollywood evangelist, or by some culturally neutered religionist. We need truth in the inner parts.

Once we begin to trace our roots as a people to the original Black Hebrew-Israelite nation our roots become extremely important. Thank God for the work of Mr. Alex Hailey, but we can trace our Biblical and spiritual roots beyond Kunte Kente and Chicken George. We can trace our roots back to Adam, Moses, to Abraham, Isaac and Jacob, to Judah, Joseph and Solomon, and ultimately to Jesus Christ.

It is very important that we find an identity with Jesus Christ that is not mediated by whites with the help of the Euro-slave Christian academy. To falsify history and blaspheme the name of God by accepting the image of Michalangelo's model as Jesus Christ betrays the arrogance, the presumptuousness of the Western status-quo. This image becomes the personification of bigotry and the ultimate symbol of Western racism. This picture of Jesus Christ and the American assumptions embodied therein has become the "golden calf" of American civil religion. We are living in a time, a Kairos, an appointed historical moment when the Father is parting the veil of history to show the light of truth. This obviously has cataclysmic implications for the Church.

Dr. Na'im Akbar has provided us with some valuable insights on the significance of historical study and perspective. He writes, "There is a certain hesitation about dwelling on events of the past. On the one hand, it creates an atmosphere of determination which removes the volitional possibilities of people to alter their condition. It tends to excuse the perpetuation of past events which could be altered simply by initiative. It preoccupies people unnecessarily and purposelessly with old hurts, tending old wounds. It is an emotional trade that ultimately provides no constructive solution for the present. But those who fail to recognize that the past is a shaper of the present, and the hand of yesterday continues to write on the slate of today, leave themselves vulnerable by not realizing the impact of influence which do serve to shape their lives." (Na'im Akbar "Claims and Images of Psychological Slavery" July 1990)

There is another poignant quote from Dr. Akbar which is essential to part of our discussion in this chapter. He states, "The slavery that captures the mind and incarcerates the motivation, perception, aspiration, and identity in a web of anti-self images, generating a personal and collective self-destruction, is more cruel than the shackles on the wrists and ankles. The slavery that feeds on the psychology invading the soul of man, destroying his loyalties to himself and establishing allegiance to forces which destroy him, is an even worse form of capture. The influences that permit an illusion of freedom, liberation, and self-determination, while tenaciously holding one's mind in subjugation is the folly of only the sadistic" (Akbar, ibid). The sadist is one who practices sadism which "Webster's New World Dictionary" defines as, "the getting of pleasure from inflicting physical or psychological pain on another or others."

Tell me a nation is "Christian" which practices sadism as a political policy with no remorse; tell me preachers are "Christians" who mount massive pro-America campaigns and respond with "let's forget the past..." when questioned regarding the incongruity between God's righteousness and American Christianity.

There is a peculiar phenomenon in the American Church that has a deliberate blind spot to issues of racism. Much of the so-called dialogue in which I have personally been involved is not dialogue at all. I remember once reading in a book by the brilliant African-American churchman and intellectual Cornel West something quite intriguing. Professor West during a trip to England was attempting to figure out what it was, in spite of all that he found contemptible about the smugness of these English people, that he appreciated. He concluded that it was the seriousness with which the English approach "engaged argument." Unfortunately in America most of the paltry amount of engaged argument that happens is in the halls of academia. This is certainly not an attack upon intellectuals nor another boring diatribe against the academy. I am simply suggesting that there need to be engaged argument regarding critical issues which involves not just academes, but pastors, church workers and church members.

The level of superficiality in the American Church is embarassing. Studies reveal an astonishing level of Biblical illiteracy among Christians and this is definitely one reason for such a noticeable absence of engaged argument at the pastoral and congregational level.

The Church, if it is to address the issues of racism not only in the culture at large, but within its own holy borders, needs a fresh hermeneutic based upon the re-telling of history. There can be no serious discussions of unity and reconciliation in the Church when the parameters are as they are. White theologians, pastors and professing believers must realize that God is a God of justice. How can we give patronizing and narcoticizing sermons about love, peace, equality, and brotherhood while keeping silent about political policies that have corralled blacks into American concentration camps called inner cities. The term inner city is by definition exclusive and segregated. It pre-supposes the existence of an outer-city. My white brothers and sisters must know that uninformed statements like "we just don't see any racism" are vacuous and irresponsible.

Curiously enough in George Barna's latest book "What Americans Believe" the statement is made relative to Black and White Christians, "Whites and Blacks have little in common when it comes to ranking life's priorities." Mr. Barna is president and founder of one of the most respected research firms in America and is a reliable source of data for such diverse firms as Visa and The Disney Channel.

Does this disparity in concern for issues of life betray

a fundamental difference in the way Black and White Christians view their Christianity and interpret their Bible? This disparity is definitely a testimony to the absence of serious and engaged argument over life issues in the Church. Blacks and Whites, with some exceptions are in their own camps doing their thing. Many Blacks who have wanted to speak out are afraid of angering Whites who will retaliate with charges of divisiveness, disunity or worse yet, demon possession. Some African-American ministers who have been raised to platforms of prominence with help from white ministers or who receive financial support from whites fear losing their platforms if they deal with truth. Many of these persons all of whom I love dearly are offering us transparent rhetoric about dialogue and unity while dealing with the split in their own consciences over their own hypocrisy and betrayal. My brothers and sisters this is a form of slavery. Studies such as Mr. Barna's indicate that strong support for many of the television and radio ministries comes from African-American Christians in the $20,000 and under annual income levels. Many of these ministries are white and scarcely if ever address the issues which continue to confront African-Americans both in and out of the Church.

For some provocative comments on our white brothers who talk of unity while upholding the status-quo which presents it we turn to once exiled Brazilian educator Paulo Freire. Professor Freire writes: "Those who promote a white theology propose an even greater passivity for the oppressed classes by disregarding the unity between reconciliation and liberation. For them the reconciliation is nothing more than the dominated acceding to the will of the dominant. All this supposes it were possible to reduce reconciliation to a kind of pact between dominant and dominated, "rich and poor".A pact that accepts the continuation of the oppressed reality in which the dominated, in return, receive efficient and modernized social assistance" (Paulo Friere, "Politics of Education" 1985). The

Church is not to be an institution of the status quo and an instrument to perpetuate ideologies or theologies of oppression and domination. Instead the Church should be unequivocally committed to extracting the purpose and affirming the dignity of every person. The Church is to be a prophetic voice for justice and peace, interpreted Biblically.

When our white brothers and sisters come to the table to participate in engaged argument they must know that we come as equals. The condescending parternalism which American culture breeds in white males must be repented of. We are not saying "you have all the answers, come help us." We are saying "we all confess Jesus Christ as Savior, our culture is sick, our nation is backslidden, come let us reason together and strategize, let us hear the voice of God, and bring repentance and deliverance first to the Church, then to the nation."

My white brothers and sisters you must sit at the feet of God's Black apostles and prophets and have the truth taught to you. We have sat and continue to sit at the feet of your teachers and prophets. We have read your history, studied your commentaries, attended your universities and churches, and helped to finance your ministries. My black brothers and sisters to whom God is given this charge you must receive and teach truth in a spirit of love and kindness. However, you must yet be firm and prophetic. "For this is the hour saith the Lord, when the veil is being drawn back and there shall come forth the light of truth. This is my working saith God and ye shall know the laborers by their fruit. Do not mistake their anger for hatred or their forcefulness for division. For I have placed a word in their mouths and it shall be heard across America, then in Europe on both sides of what was the Iron Curtain: officials of government shall call for counsel in these matters saith God, yea, they shall offer you things, accept them not saith the Spirit of God, for I Am with and will sustain thee by my power saith the Spirit of the Lord" (Oct. 10, 1991).

108

The issues of religious, social, political, educational, and economic injustice that confronts African-Americans in and out of the Church is not a Black or White issue, it is a justice issue. Our White brothers and sisters you may not excuse yourselves from addressing these issues by attempting to polarize them racially. That is ungodly and totally irresponsible. The Prophet Micah heard this word from the Lord God: "He has showed you, O man, what is good. And what does the Lord require of you? To act justly and to love mercy and to walk humble with your God (Malachi 6:8). Amos the Prophet rebukes Judah and Israel over injustice. Amos 5:11-13 says: "You trample on the poor and force him to give you grain. Therefore, though you have built stone mansions you will not live in them; though you have planted lush vineyards, you will not drink their wine. For I know how many are your offenses and how great your sins. You oppress the righteous and take bribes and you deprive the poor of justice in the courts. Therefore the prudent man keeps quiet in such time, for the times are evil."

The Bible speaks a great deal about oppression and justice. Remember, oppression is the historical psycho-spiritual, religio-economic context out of which God through Black Prophet Moses delivered Israel. God delivered Israel then altered the multiple relationships they had with their world. He gave them a new reality, altered their perceptions, gave them a fresh reference point from which to begin to look at life.

"The ministry of Moses...represents a radical break with the social reality of Pharoah's Egypt. The newness and radical innovativeness of Moses and Israel in this period can hardly be overstated...Israel can only be understood in terms of the new call of God and his assertion of an alternative social reality. Prophecy is born precisely in that moment when the emergence of social political reality is so radical and inexplicable that it has nothing less than a theological cause....The radical break of Moses and Israel from imperial reality is a two-dimensional break from both the religion of static triumphalism and the politics of oppression and exploitation." ...At the same time, Moses dismantles the politics of oppression and exploitation by countering it with a politics of justice and compassion" (Walter Bruggeman).

The above quote from Walter Bruggeman really speaks to the heart issue of this book, namely the call for a new United States of America wherein dwelleth justice and peace, righteousness and truth, mercy and equity. In Matthew 23:23 Jesus said, "Woe to you, teachers of the law and Pharisees, you hypocrites! You give a tenth of your spices-mint, dill and cumin. But you have neglected the more important matters of the law-justice, mercy and faithfulness." I like the late Paul Tillich's notion of justice. In volume three of Tillich's "Systemic Theology" he defines justice as "...the aim of all cultural actions which are directed toward the transformation of society. The word can also apply to the individual, in so far as he behaves in a just way. But more frequently another term, namely, righteous, is used in this sense: he who is righteous exercises Justice" (Paul Tillich, "Systematic Theology" 1963, p. 66). Karen Lebacqz has written: "The grounding of justice in remembrance means that human justice can never be separated from God's actions. Human justice is born in relationship with God. Human justice is always a response to God's interventions. Rather than turning to human laws or human reason for a theory of justice, we must turn to God" (Lebacqz 1987).

An element of Catholic polity which I deeply respect is the willingness of Catholic clergy, priests, bishops, archbishops, etc. to interface, to dialogue with contemporary issues and summarize their conclusions in position papers. They are willing to embrace the tension between theology and the contemporary world and in some cases even to jettison outdated theological assumptions. There needs to be more of this kind of dialogue among Protestant theologians and clergy in the U.S. and the so-called Third World.

On the subject of justice, there needs to be dialogue. We

have an understanding of what injustice was in the agricultural and industrial ages, but what about in the Information Age? What contours will injustice take in the Information Age in the Global Community? What will global oppression, information oppression look like? What does it look like? What are the distinguishing features? The old wine of white Protestant academic slave theology must be born-again to speak a credible Word from God into such a system of exponentially changing complexities.

Let us confront straight on Christianity's loss of credibility across the landscape of America and most of the world. Islam is the world's fastest growing religion today covering over a third of the globe. Again I quote Karen Labacqz, "Christianity has become an instrument for cultural suppression and alienation. In the eyes of oppressed peoples around the world, Christianity has become identified with cultural imperialism. It preaches the "derision and arrogance" of the West instead of the compassion of the gospel (Lebacqz 1987). Ms. Lebacqz further states: "Christianity was brought to Africa, Asia, and Latin American "wrapped in Western culture and Western values." The values of Western culture were thereafter presented as the values of Christian faith. Christians looked at-and judged-other people through Western eyes. This faith became "ideological" identified with the ideologies of the West" (ibid).

I am in no way anti-American. I too have been at times mesmerized by the grandeur of her pageantry, swooned by the rhetoric of her great political documents." O beautiful for spacious skies, for amber waves of grain. For purple mountains majesty above the fruited plain. America, America, God shed His grace on thee. And crown thy good with brotherhood from sea to shining sea." I sang that with such passion in the early years of my life. Now I see a generation of African-American and other ethnic children who are cynical of America's songs, pledges, and promises long before their teen years.

111

American pastors please hear the cry of my heart. God is giving us space to repent and to issue a prophetic plea to the Church to confront that which opposes the very character and nature of God. The Church must tear itself away from its status quo moorings and commit to the prophetic purposes of the One, True, Living, and Just God or risk being vomited from His mouth as a puny, putrid, and irrelevant imposter.

We in the American Church must comprehensively grasp racism, sexism, classism, injustice and oppression. We must eschew simplistic or individualistic pseudo solutions and grapple in prayer and dialogue with the enormity and spiritual implications of these issues. We must come together in serious Bible study listening for and discerning the prophetic voice of Scripture. Trained pastors and theologians must begin to listen to the cry of the people and where necessary help them to rebuild their shattered yet priceless human dignity.

In a stirring little book "Bible of the Oppressed" Elsa Tamez writes, "There is almost a complete absence of the theme of oppression in European and North American Biblical theology. But the absence is not suprising, since it is possible to tackle this theme only with an existential situation of oppression" (Tamez 1982). "Webster's New World Dictionary" defines existential as "of based on, or expressing existence" i.e., one must live in the immediate context of oppression as a member of the oppressed class to properly theologize regarding oppression. This certainly is not the case with most Europeans, North American theologians and seminarians. This would include theologians of color who have uncritically accepted the tenets of the Western theological academy.

Let us look at a few of the Hebrew words taken from Professor Tamez's work. These words deal with oppression.

1.) anah: degradation of the human person; affects the inmost being of the person; tyranny of the powerful; sexual violation of a woman

2.) ashaq: violent despoliation and consequent impoverishment of the oppressed; ruthless violence

3.) lahats: the smashing blow of the oppressor and the immediate outcry of the oppressed

4.) nagash: violent exploitation, chiefly by means of forced labor; compulsion to produce; pressure from the oppressor

5.) yanah: deadly violence used for the despoliation of the poor; exploitation in the form of enslavement; fraud

6.) ratsats: crushing and despoiling of the poor

7.) daka': the grinding effect of oppression that penetrates the whole person, oppression interiorly as well as exteriorly; a knocking down

8.) dak: vexation of the poor, the persistent hope of the poor for the establishment of a new and just order

9.) tok: the tyranny of the oppressor, exercised in deceit

Professor Tamez writes, "The underlying cause of oppression is the desire to pile up riches; this explains the repeated appearance of despoliation and theft (Tamez 1982). I would add to Professor Tamez's comments that the piling up of riches is not an end in itself. Perhaps this point is obvious perhaps not. The lording of riches allows the oppressor class to maintain the structures of power and the nature of these structures with their relationship to the oppressed. The consequences of this are far reaching.

Thomas W. Ogletree in "Hospitality to the Stronger" gives in insightful definition of oppression. He writes, "To be oppressed is to be virtually without a home. It is not only to be structured vulnerable to those who wield power; it is also to be forced to work out a sense of self within a context determined by the definitions, priorities and interests of the oppressor. One's own stories are continually recast and reassessed in the interpretation of the oppressor. They are changed into charming little playlets which offer comic relief within the great aromatic movement of reigning social stories. It is highly unlikely that persons who fare well in an oppressive social system will by themselves discover anything problematic about that system. The system will seem more or less "natural" and altogether inevitable. if anything new is to emerge, it will arise though the iniatives of the oppressed, assisted perhaps by a few class traitors" (Ogletree 1985).

Please read over Professor Ogletree's definition of oppression. He suggests that some will view the oppressive society as "altogether inevitable." This is double-mindedness for the Christian. To assume inevitability in the societal realm as it relates to oppression is to adopt a determinism which the same Christians would uncategorically reject in the moral and ethical realm. Determinism, simply stated is a philosophical notion which suggests that events are pre-programmed into the form and function of the universe and that human beings are not responsible for them thus not morally accountable for them. This would be a convenient escape if it were true, however, it is not. Human beings are responsible for oppression, injustice, racism, sexism, and classism. Human beings are also accountable to God and one another for these transgressions.

As we approach the end of this book, I would like to comment on President Bush's New World Order specifically as it relates to Africa. In a recent magazine article Mulinde Musoke stated, "This is a crucial period for Africa, when its marginalization in geopolitics and economic affairs reached a new high. When President Bush expressed his vision of the "new world order" Africa was hardly mentioned" (World Press Review 1991 p. 11).

In the same magazine there is an article by Gamini Ueerakoon entitled "Africa No Longer a Proxy for the Superpowers." In the article the author writes, "The Horn of Africa appears to have lost much of its strategic value to the U.S. and the U.S.S.R. The Soviet Union lost South Yemen when North and South Yemen united last year. When the lease on the Berbera base expired last year, the U.S. did not bother to renegotiate it, and when Siad Barre was threatened by rebels, there was no response from the U.S. The fall of pro-U.S. and Pro-Soviet dictators and diminishing strategic interests will certainly bring about a radical transformation in the politics of the African continent."

In a recent book Marvin Certon and Owen Davies have

written: "To say the least, Africa has been badly served by its colonial history. The borders drawn by European powers, like those in the Middle East, did not create true nation-states, where people linked by similar ethnic or cultural backgrounds can manage their affairs as a relatively homogenous group. Instead they forced native people together without regard for tribal identities and animosities. This has permanently scarred African politics" (Marvin Certon and Owen Davies 1991).

Though I am by no means placing all of the burden for Africa's enormous political, social, economic, and health upon Western nations they clearly are largely responsible. Many of the brutal African dictatorships of the" independence era " were propped up by Western governments. Were it not for Africa and other parts of the Third World, the United States and other Western nations could never build the ecomonic empires which survive today. Recent studies indicate that twenty-four of the world's twenty-six drastically indebted low-income countries are in Africa. Many African countries have become addicted to aid. It is the moral responsibility of the West to assist with developing those African countries systemically underdeveloped by capitalistic greed and Western imperialism. This does not only involve money but the West must accept responsibility for political vacuum and internal political reactionism directly related to Western politics.

Our concerns are not limited to Africa but also to Latin America. To Argentina, Brazil, Mexico, Columbia, Bolivia, El Salvador, Venezuela, etc., our compassion also extends to the Third World in America; to so-called Urban communities (ghet-colonies) in Dallas, Los Angeles, Detroit, Brooklyn, Seattle, Philadelphia, Chicago and so on.

In my local newspaper dated Monday, January 14, 1991 there was an article entitled "Deepening Racism Threatens Nation, Church Leaders Warn." I quote the following from the aforementioned article: "Racist attitudes...permeate most of our institutions and systematic racism underlies economic and social disparities between whites and non-whites. As a result of racial discrimination, all over the United States there are 'quiet riots' in the form of unemployment, poverty, social disorganization, family disintegration, housing and school deterioration and crime..."

In 1991 many major national news magazines featured cover stories dealing with race and racism. Newsweek, May 6, 1991 are just a couple of examples. The same two national news magazines carried cover stories addressing the African origins of civilization.

The White church, white Christian leaders, writers, pastors, television and media personnel can no longer turn deaf ears, blind eyes, and cold hearts toward the rampant injustice which pervades great America. There is a seething anger, a deep despair rising out of Urban America. Many have lost faith in God and in the Church inasmuch as they view the Church not as the prophetic mouthpiece of God but as an arm of right wing party politics.

This discussion must not be reduced to the tactic of holding up one brother or sister of color as a validation of the systems effectiveness. This is deceptive, plays to capitalistic individualism and ignores structural and systematic injustice. This Western society with its racism, sexism, classism, international terrorism and exploitation, dehumanizing school systems and manipulative media is crushing the spirits and bruising the humanity of millions. Our cry to them is up from the dust! Let us cry to the God of Abraham, Isaac, and Jacob. The God of the Hebrew-Israelite nation. From our pulpits and with every tool available we must begin to prophetically enter America's waste places. We must preach self-definition, dignity, and self-respect. The scourge of drugs, violence, black on black crime, despair, cynicism and resignation must be countered with hope.

God is not America's God, He is not the white man's God. He is the God of justice, He is the God of the oppressed.

The Church is the Body of Christ, made in His image. Jesus bowels ached over the oppression, sickness, disease, and alienation He witnessed. He was not the apolitical disengaged status quo guru that much of the Western theological and hermeneutical approach conveys. He spoke of a kingdom wherein is justice, righteousness, and redemption. Wherein is healing, salvation and relocation. This Jesus embraced lepers, conversed with prostitutes, stood in solidarity with the outcasts of His day. He has a word for the waste places of America at the dawning of the 21st century. "The Spirit of the Lord is upon me; he has anointed me to preach Good News to the poor; he has sent me to heal the brokenhearted and to announce that captives shall be released and the blind shall see, that the downtrodden shall be freed from their oppressors and that God is ready to give blessings to all who come to him" (Luke 4:18,19 TLB).

This work is not exhaustive, nor shall it be my last. The writing has been a deeply emotional experience for me. I have not tried to hide my anger though my anger should not be construed as hatred, hostility, anti-white or anything other than anger. An anger motivated by a passionate love for the Lord and for His people of all colors, cultures, and tongues. I am sure that many of us share a vexation and spiritual anguish over the superficiality, hypocrisy and division at large in the society and church. As the pastor of a cultural diverse fellowship of Blacks, Whites, Asians and Mexican-Americans I long for the true communion of the saints.

I embrace all the Body of Christ with our varying, yet rich traditions, and am committed to true healing and unity. I fundamentally subscribe to all that is noble and just in America's creeds and canons. I believe in a truly just and flourishing market economy that fully utilizes and recognizes the various skills and gifts of America's beautifully diverse populace. I believe in a strong and prosperous America from now until Jesus Christ returns. However, in order for this to happen dignity, justice, and prosperity for all must now become the goal of the Kingdom of God. No ghettoes, welfare, federally funded abortions, non-existent venture capital, hopelessness and lack of vision. This is not a time for discouragement. This is the

hour of vision, lofty purpose, commitment, and self-sacri-
fice. Let us all black, brown, red, yellow, and white, rebuild
the waste places of America and the world; restoring a
people to dignity and true freedom. We hear the eternally
prophetic voice of the Master as He declares," And ye shall
know the truth, and the truth shall make you free."

There is something deeply personal about writing and
one runs the risk of being misunderstood however, I feel
the risk has been necessary. The silence, my personal
silence had to be broken. In his book "Finally Comes the
Poet" Walter Brueggeman has written: "It is speech that
binds God and human creatures. The preaching task is to
guide people out of the alienated silence of exaggerated
self, and out of the silence of denial and rage of an exaggerated God, into a serious, dangerous, subversive, coven-
tal conversation, a conversation that is the root forum of
communion. Communion is not possible where speech is
destroyed either by selfishness or by submissiveness. In
the midst of these reductions, the preacher is invited to
speak in ways that open a world of conversation, commu-
nication, and communion."

So our conversation has begun. May it be carried on
with hearing ears, compassionate hearts, and enflamed
minds in a spirit of mutual understanding and respect.
Peace be with you.

November 1, 1991
Bremerton, Wa.

Select Bibliography

Birley, Anthony R. (1972) — Septimius Severus: The African Emperor, Yale University Press

Bohannan, Paul; Curtin, Philip (1988) — Africa and Africans, Waveland Press

Davidson, Basil (1969) — The African Genius, Little Brown and Company

Davidson, Basil (1959) — The Lost Cities of Africa, Little Brown and Company

Diop, Cheikh Anta (1975) — The African Origin of Civilization, Lawrence Hill & Company

DuBois, William E.B. (1965) — The World and Africa, International Publishers

Edwards, Jefferson D. (1989) — Chosen Not Cursed, Vincom, Inc.

Franklin, John Hope (1947) — From Slavery to Freedom, Alfred A. Knopf, Inc.

Frazier, E. Franklin (1964) — The Negro Church in America, Schocken Books

Hansberry, William Leo (1974) — Pillars in Ethiopian History Volume I, Howard University Press

Hansberry, William Leo (1977) — Africa and Africans Volume II, Howard University Press

Hastings, Adrian (1976) — African Christianity, The Seabury Press

Houston, Drusilla Dunjee (1926) — Wonderful Ethiopians of the Ancient Cushite Empire, Black Classic Press

Herodotus — The Histories, Penguin Classics

Hyman, Mark (1983) — Blacks Who Died for Jesus, Winston-Derek Publishers, Inc.

Jackson, John (1933, 1987) — Was Jesus Christ a Negro, ECA Associates

Jackson, John (1970) — Introduction to African Civilizations, Citadel Press

Johnson, J.C. deGraft (1986) — African Glory, Black Classic Press

Johnson, John L. (1991) — The Black Biblical Heritage, Winston-Derek Publishers, Inc.

Jones, Major J. (1987) — The Color of God, Mercer University Press

Khamit-Kush, Indus (1983) — What They Never Told You in History Class, Luxorr Publications

McCray, Rev. Walter A. — The Black Presence in the Bible Volumes I & II, Black Light Fellowship

Mazrui, Ali A (1986) — The Africans, Little, Brown and Company

Mosley, William (1987) — What Color Was Jesus, African American Images

Sanneh, Lamin (1983) — West African Christianity, Orbis Books

Ullendorff, Edward (1968) — Ethiopia and the Bible Oxford University Press

Van Sertima, Ivan (1989) — Egypt Revisited, Transaction Publishers

Van Sertima, Ivan (1986) — Great African Thinkers Volume I, Transaction Books

Wessels, Anton (1990) — Images of Jesus, William B. Eerdmans

Williams, Chancellor (1987) — The Destruction of Black Civilization, Third World Press

Williams, George W. (Reprint 1989) — History of the Negro Race in America Volume I and II, The Ayer Company, Publishers

For Additional Copies of

AND YE SHALL KNOW THE TRUTH
or

To inquire concerning Pastor Giles'
teaching, preaching, and workshop itinerary;
or to inquire concerning other
audio-learning systems by the author.

Contact:
New Life World Ministries
P.O. Box 465
Bremerton, Washington 98310

(206) 373-0901

Cover Art by Craig Williams of Craig's Creations
Photography by Anita Perrine

About the Author

James L. Giles is president of New Life World Ministries and co-pastor, along with his wife, Shelley, of New Life Family Christian Center, an interdenominational, multi-ethnic church in Bremerton, Washington. He has studied philosophy, history, and sociology, at the University of Washington in Seattle. Pastor Giles is a two-term gubernatorial appointee to Washington State's historic nine member Commission on African-American Affairs. He has lectured in African history at institutes of higher learning and was a featured speaker and panelist for the School of Public Health and Community Medicine at the University of Washington School of Medicine in 1992. Pastor Giles is also the author of "The God Factor," and "The Essence of Greatness." He is the author/presenter of workshops in the area of human potential, and is in increasing demand as a prophetic teacher, exhorter, and motivator. Pastor Giles and his wife, Shelley are the parents of four sons; Cedric, Armand, Stephen, and Langston; their Four Kings.